Teaching Poetry, Embracing Perspectives

Teaching Poetry, Embracing Perspectives

A Guide for Middle School Teachers

Sharon Discorfano

ROWMAN & LITTLEFIELD
Lanham • Boulder • New York • London

Published by Rowman & Littlefield
A wholly owned subsidiary of The Rowman & Littlefield Publishing Group, Inc.
4501 Forbes Boulevard, Suite 200, Lanham, Maryland 20706
www.rowman.com

Unit A, Whitacre Mews, 26-34 Stannary Street, London SE11 4AB

British Library Cataloguing in Publication Information Available

Library of Congress Cataloging-in-Publication Data

Names: Discorfano, Sharon, 1970- author.
Title: Teaching poetry, embracing perspectives : a guide for middle school
    teachers / Sharon Discorfano.
Description: Lanham, Maryland : Rowman & Littlefield, 2017.
Identifiers: LCCN 2017020933 (print) | LCCN 2017035763 (ebook) | ISBN
    9781475835373 (electronic) | ISBN 9781475835359 (cloth : alk. paper) |
    ISBN 9781475835366 (pbk. : alk. paper)
Subjects: LCSH: Poetry—Study and teaching (Middle school)—United States. |
    Creative writing (Middle school)—United States.
Classification: LCC LB1631 (ebook) | LCC LB1631 .D56 2017 (print) | DDC
    808.10712—dc23
LC record available at https://lccn.loc.gov/2017020933

∞™ The paper used in this publication meets the minimum requirements of
American National Standard for Information Sciences—Permanence of Paper
for Printed Library Materials, ANSI/NISO Z39.48-1992.

Printed in the United States of America

For my nephew
(and favorite middle schooler),
Nicholas

Contents

Preface

Although everyone expects some poetry instruction in high school and college classes, most schools are hesitant about giving it any in-depth study during the middle school stage. However, during the two years I spent teaching twelve-year-old boys, I discovered that not only are students at this age capable, but they also are at the *ideal* age for an introduction to sophisticated poetry. They, like high school students, can benefit a great deal from studying poetry and exploring poetry writing as a form of expression.

Developmentally, middle school students are right on the cusp of starting to think more abstractly. In addition, poetry characteristically expresses complex emotions that they are just starting to experience for themselves. In this sense, it can be a comfort to them to know the feelings they are experiencing, perhaps for the first time, are shared by others; and the use of metaphors becomes an accessible, effective way for them to articulate ideas swirling around in their heads as they are entering the tough teen years. In this respect, teachers of poetry can provide their students with another useful tool as they confront issues pervading our society, both within and beyond the classroom walls.

Unfortunately, I've encountered many teachers who are hesitant about incorporating a formal study of poetry into their curriculum, aside from perhaps a perfunctory poetry unit. Some teachers have expressed a concern that poetry will be intimidating, if not boring, to their students; or, they have shared with me that poetry is a bit out of their own comfort zone, not having taken many poetry classes as part of their own undergraduate or graduate studies.

I decided to undertake the writing of this book because I believe in the benefits of poetry study—particularly for middle school students, for the reasons mentioned above—as well as high school students. Moreover, I believe teachers, through poetry, can help students discover how diversity adds, rather than detracts, from our life experiences; and this understanding is especially crucial in light of our polarized political climate these days. Different voices, different perspectives—not only are they worthy of our consideration and respect, but they also have the potential to add another dimension to our own experience of the world as we walk through it each day.

In class, students will listen to their classmates form their own interpretations of the same poem; they will learn that there are many ways of looking at the same thing and the value of having multiple viewpoints to consider at the same time. They will learn through experience that multiple views should not be thought of as ideas competing against each other, with only one possible winner in the bunch. Rather, competing ideas get us to think in ways we have not thought before and *that* is exciting. And when the time comes for them to write and share their own poems, and for listening to others respond to their work, students will learn the value of mutual support and the benefits of an atmosphere of mutual respect.

The greatest gift a teacher gives is helping a student to bloom. The greatest gift a teacher gets is the privilege of helping a student to bloom. It is especially rewarding when a teacher can be there to see it happening. It is my hope that, in sharing this program with other teachers, I am extending such gifts to you.

Acknowledgments

Any teacher will understand why the first people I need to thank are my students. Teaching is hard work, but it also is such a privilege to spend our days in the classroom sharing with others what is important and exciting to us. There is nothing quite like witnessing a student's sense of wonder and the thrill of discovery. So, I thank all my students—some younger, some older— not only for their efforts, but also for their energizing effect on me and for keeping me learning.

My respect and gratitude to my former students at St. David's School during the two years I developed this poetry program: thank you for embracing the challenges of poetry and meeting each task with honesty and enthusiasm. Watching you develop as readers and writers and tap into your own creativity was one of the greatest rewarding experiences I have had as a teacher. Special thanks to: Ben Lindbergh, Andrew Kitirattragarn, Peter MacDonald, Justin Church, Jed Kelly, Cannon Skidmore, Martin Ambrose, John Hannon, Keats Sexton, Charlie Allen, Loukiano Stavrinos, Justin Church, Antonio Brecevich, Luiz Felipe Das Neves, Sam Fryer, and Alex Bongard (in memoriam).

Thank you to all my teachers and mentors throughout the years, in and out of the classroom. I would especially like to acknowledge Dr. Katharine Wallingford and the impact she had on me as a teacher, writer, and person: as a freshman in college, you gave me my first real glimpse of what poetry had to offer; you continued to nurture my understanding throughout my college years, and I couldn't have asked for a greater role model or source of inspiration as a young woman, still a little shaky in my confidence and skills. Also, I am indebted to Susan Wood for inviting me to discover poetry writing in a more formal way as part of her poetry class at Rice University, where I first experienced the supportive "safe" workshop environment that I advocate for in these pages.

To my teaching colleagues throughout the years who played such an important role in making my day-to-day as a teacher such a rewarding experience: your insights, support, and friendship have been a blessing.

Finally, to everyone at Rowman & Littlefield for believing in this book, and especially Sarah Jubar, Carlie Wall, and Megan DeLancey for adding their expertise, diligence, and kindness to the mix.

Introduction

The function of education is to teach one to think intensively and to think critically. Intelligence plus character—that is the goal of true education.

—*Martin Luther King, Jr.*

Whatever direction our lives take, in terms of being considered a well-rounded, educated person, we are expected to have at least a small storehouse in mind of the most frequently anthologized poems. But what is it about poetry that makes it so invaluable as a way of preparing for other, apparently unrelated, fields? Is it worthwhile? Useful? And, if so, in what ways? As we are thrust forward at light speed using the latest technologies, why are we still reading Wordsworth?

This book serves as a theoretical and practical guide, appropriate for teachers of middle school students as well as higher grade levels, and provides clear and fully developed lesson plans and activities teachers can follow. In many respects, the program's aims are comparable to other English curricula: introducing students to works in the canon as well as to multicultural texts; refining critical reading and writing skills; and the development of abstract thinking and interpretation. However, the program detailed in these pages goes a step further, and perhaps has even greater relevance today than ever. In this book, we have a second, larger purpose: using poetry as a vehicle for developing students' awareness of multiple perspectives and an appreciation for diversity.

What follows is an easy-to-implement program, including a selection of poems that have proven successful for this age level. At the core of the program is a straightforward, four-step method of analysis, offered here with detailed lesson plans. The lessons build on each other to effectively hone analytical skills while at the same time reaching for the stated, larger objective of the program (*The Bigger Picture*). The second part of the program, where students take on the role of poetry writers, complements the first part on both of these levels.

Whatever background teachers have in poetry, they can use the program described in these pages to create stimulating and productive classes that will help students develop their interpretive skills within the larger framework of developing their awareness; and, in doing so, we hope students will become more compassionate human beings.

So, back to the original queston. What's so special about poetry? What makes it relevant and still a worthwhile study? As a means of developing one's critical reading skills, the analysis of a poem is the ideal vehicle, partially because of its brevity. Abstract thinking and analysis is exhausting work, especially when students are just starting out. Any reading assignment that requires more than looking up objective answers to comprehension questions—when done *right*—demands that the students be alert and focused in order to absorb literal details and shape them into something meaningful.

Poems, and therefore reading assignments in a poetry program, are typically going to be shorter in length than an average night's reading assignment when a class is working its way through a novel or collection of short stories. Poetry's condensed language prevents students from feeling like they are drowning in words and paragraphs and pages, so they can more readily zero in on the details. Furthermore, the brevity of a poem allows for repeated reading, which is essential for the construction of a fluid interpretation. In this program, students are asked to read an assigned poem at least three times. And the length of the average poem is not the only thing that makes it more manageable: generally, poems will adhere to one main idea or a few related images, making it easier for students to attempt a close textual reading while still addressing broader universal themes.

In addition, by using poetry, a teacher can focus on just one or two literary devices a poem exemplifies and, in this way, incrementally expand the students' critical vocabulary to include terms they will find useful in their own future analyses. Increasing students' confidence when it comes to developing interpretive skills and giving them the language they will need to express their ideas are the keys to success of any literature program, whatever the age level of the student.

HOW TO CHOOSE POEMS FOR CLASS

In selecting poems to use in class, teachers should note that narrative poems—poems that tell some story—tend to be the most accessible, and the young student can usually find something in them he can relate to: a victory, a parent-child relationship, a feeling of fear, and so forth. In addition to focusing on narrative poems, a teacher would do well to choose poems that are simple in their language, such as the ones by Gwendolyn Brooks and William Carlos Williams provided here. In doing so, she or he will help students quickly set aside any notion of poetry as a bunch of lofty, rhyming words; poetry will not only seem more accessible to them, but also more relevant.

Whatever poems a teacher decides on, it is best to keep in mind that, while younger students can tackle challenging poems, they should do fewer of them. So, instead of four or five poems a night, assign them just one or two. Trying to get them to do any more than this will only result in less-focused reading, analysis, and discussions. However, in order to effectively monitor students and ensure that they are, in fact, putting in the time and necessary energy, teachers should require students each night to record their thought processes in a writing notebook in which they document their working through the four-step method of this program for each poem assigned.

POETRY WRITING ASSIGNMENTS

Besides having shorter reading assignments, students are likely to have shorter writing assignments for awhile. As they are learning to think abstractly, and as they are learning how to incorporate textual evidence so that the essay still flows, shorter writing assignments of just one or a few paragraphs are, in the long run, more fruitful than full-length essays at the onset.

It is important to challenge students in manageable increments that will allow for a gradual increase in confidence as well as ability. Several short writing assignments will give students time to focus on just a few elements at a time and demand from them a close textual analysis—and will not put them in the overwhelming position of having to come up with a string of paragraphs to form a cohesive argument early on. Assigned prematurely, a lengthy assignment could scare away students from poetry and writing permanently.

Finally, shorter writing assignments will allow the teacher to provide more immediate and thorough feedback that, in turn, students will be able to more easily digest and put into practice moving forward.

ADDITIONAL BENEFITS OF
READING AND WRITING POETRY

On a different yet very practical level, teaching poetry also serves as an excellent way to help gear up students for the inevitable series of standardized tests they will encounter during their academic careers. The study of poetry, and the development of critical reading and analytical skills that comes with it, can enhance a student's performance on such tests—most specifically, in response to comprehension questions focusing on details, themes, or tone. To further reinforce the test-taking skills to be gained from poetry study, a teacher can incorporate into the syllabus some very specific practice by creating mock standardized-test questions based on any poems discussed in class. Examples of this kind of exercise are included in this book.

Beyond its focus on developing a student's skills as a critical reader, integral to this program is its second half, at which point students take on the role of poetry writer: they will be experimenting with different poetic forms, and the classroom transforms into a workshop environment. At this stage, students learn first-hand the thrill of creativity and possibilities of figurative language. In the process, they develop a better appreciation of the challenges in creating a fresh perspective and working toward greater precision in language in order to best articulate their view.

CONNECTIONS TO A BIGGER PICTURE

But, again, the aim of this program is twofold; and the writing portion of the program speaks to the second, larger, purpose as well. By emphasizing the plurality of views and encouraging us to get beyond the concrete, literal aspects of something, poetry encourages us to think on a more abstract level in our own daily lives. Poetry helps us to make connections between what seem disparate things and to recognize underlying motivations for things that are not immediately apparent to us.

In this way, poetry has the potential to teach us all how to be more human. It allows us not only to express, but also to experience, the universality of the human condition. Especially in this day and age, one could argue that a primary goal of all education—whether in English class, history, or even science—must be to instill our future generations with a sense of compassion, responsibility, and unity as members of the human race. Ultimately, this is the goal.

In sum, the following poetry program, which incorporates both analysis and creative writing, provides a teacher with an opportunity to have the impact so many of us strive for throughout our careers as educators. In addition to the knowledge we are imparting to students—in itself, a wonderful gift—we are helping individuals develop self-awareness and alternative modes of expression; simultaneously, we are fostering in students a respect for the views of others and how someone chooses to articulate those views. The classroom becomes a place that doesn't just tolerate or appreciate diversity—it thrives on it. The classroom becomes a garden of creativity. The classroom becomes a community.

Poetry and a Few Hot Topics

The ultimate goal of this program as it has been designed is far-reaching: beyond poetry for poetry's sake and the enrichment it offers to any individual who gives it serious study, we are using poetry at this stage of students' development to underscore the value in appreciating the validity of multiple perspectives and in respecting the diversity around them. This awareness is something students will carry with them into their daily lives, and it has direct relevance to "hot topics" of the day. A few for any teacher to consider and possibly address within their own school community include those that follow.

ANTI-BULLYING EFFORTS

Especially in recent years, much has been written on the issue of bullying—whether on the playground, in the classroom, or via social media. There have been many commendable outreach and educational programs, media presentations, and increasing efforts by legislators and lawmakers to address bullying and cyberbullying through the legal system. When teaching poetry, here are a few points to consider:

1. The poems and range of perspectives themselves will help children better appreciate diversity.
2. By developing their capacity to experience the other—seeing the world or an event through the speaker's eyes/words—a student becomes more adept at putting himself in another's shoes in real life situations.
3. In writing poetry, students may discover themselves in a vulnerable space they have not inhabited before, which will make them better appreciate when others find themselves in vulnerable positions.

4. Seeing classmates working diligently as they try to figure out a poem, or expressing themselves in poetic form, will get a student to see his or her friends in a different light (often, stripped of the persona they have created for themselves within the parameters of what is considered "cool" or acceptable).
5. Any projects where students are working together toward a creative end will foster a sense of camaraderie and esprit de corps.

TRANSGENDER, IDENTITY, AND SEXUALITY

One of the most controversial topics of late, especially in the school context, has been surrounding an expansion of our understanding of gender and identity. While arguments over specifics such as bathroom access continue, the takeaway here is that the next generations are framing gender and identity as a more fluid construct than it has been in the past—or, at least, more nuanced and complex than the binary familiar to preceding generations. Although this is more of a high school topic, teachers of middle school students need to be aware that this age group is on the cusp of that awakening into young adulthood. The middle school years are setting the stage for how these students will handle what is just around the corner—for each of them and for their friends.

By imparting to students the skill to recognize and appreciate perspectives and what may be labeled by others as "divergent" choices, a teacher helps prepare students for the time when these differences begin surfacing in their own immediate sphere. As a result, students will be better equipped to react with fairness and respect rather than out of fear or panic or defensiveness, which—unfortunately—often translates into alienation or aggression.

What is most important for students to learn is that difference does not mean a threat to their own views or choices. That someone else has a different view or makes a different choice does not necessarily undermine their own. This lesson is important not just for adolescence, but it is one that students, we hope, will carry with them into adulthood. A more inclusive worldview, ultimately, will enable each student to develop and maintain a healthy self-image; just as important, it will give him or her the capability to nurture healthy, mature friendships and working relationships with others.

THE ENVIRONMENT AND ANIMAL WELFARE

Fostering a deeper appreciation for multiple perspectives is not limited to just the perspectives of other human beings. A higher goal of developing sensitivities and creating more empathic human beings means fostering an awareness that is truly all-inclusive: namely, an awareness that takes equally into account the perspectives of the environment and animals. Poetry, in this sense, often gives a voice to the voiceless.

In environmental law circles, there is a seminal piece titled "Should Trees Have Standing?"[1] The question points to a legal issue created out of the fact that only a person who suffers an injury has "standing" to bring a case before the court. In other words, if you yourself have not suffered a specific injury as a result of some action, you cannot make a claim. So, should a tree that is harmed—for instance, by a company that has decided to build a resort on the land where it is rooted—have "standing" to try and stop that building from happening? Or should a person be allowed to initiate a lawsuit on the tree's behalf, without having experienced an injury herself?

The issue of standing—for a tree or an animal—is for another book, but the question is relevant here because it points to an area that, especially in recent decades, our society has expressed should matter to all of us. As Joyce Kilmer once put so simply and eloquently in his 1913 poem: "I think that I shall never see / A poem lovely as a tree." In poetry, not only marginalized human voices, but also voices of a tree, wildlife, or even a companion animal can find expression and, therefore, are perspectives worthy of consideration that can enrich our own.

NOTE

1. Christopher D. Stone, "Should Trees Have Standing? Toward Legal Rights for Natural Objects," *Southern California Law Review* 45 (1972): 450–501.

Part I

READING POEMS

While many teachers find it enriching to delve into the lives of poets and the circumstances surrounding the birth of a particular poem, this program encourages you to avoid attaching historical context to the poems at the beginning stages of the program; opportunities to weave together literary works and history or social issues will come later. At the start, it will be important to keep the focus on sharpening a student's ability to analyze a given subject as objectively as possible, with as disciplined and uniform an approach as possible. The reading and interpretation process provides a structure that students can use as a launching pad and also can fall back on as a guide or source of support when they are feeling less sure of themselves.

Students invariably express immediate delight when they glance over a syllabus and see that they only have a few pages assigned to them for the night's homework. However, after one follow-up lesson, they quickly learn the difference between reading and *critical* reading. Not only are students expected to know all of the vocabulary contained within the poem(s) and have a basic idea of what is literally happening within the poem(s); they also are expected to come into class prepared to engage in a thoughtful discussion of the images and themes each poem brings to light.

So where to begin? As with almost any other major undertaking, making that first step into the process often is the most difficult. A student may open up to the pages assigned, read a long list of words that only vaguely seem to fit together, and come to the conclusion that they still do not have any idea whatsoever what the poem is all about. And so, students are left befuddled or overwhelmed, and teachers face blank stares and frustrated minds. However, equipped with just a few simple steps, even the most perplexing poems become at least manageable, and even the student who struggles the most will find him- or herself able to make some headway.

ANALYZING A POEM (THE FOUR STEPS)

It is best to repeat these steps over and over again with students so that the process becomes second nature to them. No matter how simple the poem, we still walk through the steps.

Step 1: Vocabulary Words

Objective: Circle any words whose meaning is uncertain (either an unknown vocabulary word or a word that seems to be used in a way that is different from its usual meaning).

Read the poem straight through (preferably out loud to oneself). From the start, it is important to read the poem with attention to punctuation and grammar so that the sentences or phrases make sense to the reader.

Once all of the unknown/uncertain words have been identified, each student should refer to a dictionary of his own (a must!) and find the appropriate definitions. In this exercise, students are expanding their vocabulary by learning new words; moreover, by seeing new words in context, they are more likely to retain the knowledge and be better able to use these words themselves in the future. Furthermore, starting out with this focus on individual word choices highlights the importance of precision in language: often, it will be a secondary meaning for a word that proves more helpful than the first or more commonly used one.

After the words have been identified and supplanted with synonyms or meanings the students can comprehend and work with more readily in building an interpretation of the poem as a whole, you can move on to the next step.

Step 2: Literal

Objective: To ascertain what is *literally* happening within the poem.

Read the poem again, straight through. Once students have read through the poem a second time (perhaps somewhat more slowly and carefully this time), they should try to *paraphrase*, in the poem's margins, the literal content of the poem. Depending on the poem's length and structure, a teacher may encourage students to paraphrase each stanza, or perhaps paraphrase every few lines. Their paraphrasing will help them to process the literal circumstances—to "map out" the poem so that they are, in effect, creating a guide for themselves (in their own language) to the poem.

Unless they are using borrowed textbooks, encourage students to write directly alongside the text. First, marking up a text is a specific and essential skill in and of itself; and second, marking up a text in this way makes it easier to follow subsequent readings and to work during any time spent with the text while writing about it. Finally, the physical act of marking up a text reinforces the *active* role of the reader when it comes to interpreting a poem. For teachers whose classes are using borrowed books, it is worthwhile to make photocopies of a few included poems in order to allow students some practice in marking up a text.

The ulterior motive here is to underscore this second step as an *interim* stage of deciphering—it is not equivalent to "figuring out" the poem, but merely a necessary preliminary step on the road to forming an interpretation. Thus, the difference between literal and abstract.

It is also after the second reading of the poem that students can begin to consider basic questions:

1. Who is the speaker? (age, gender, culture/ethnicity, etc.)
2. Where is the speaker in relation to the action of the poem? (detached observer, present participant, past participant)
3. What is the time period during which the poem takes place? (season, year, era; past/present/future)
4. Is there a particular audience being addressed?

Step 3: Figurative Language

Objective: Identify images, events, or actions in the poem that will translate into an abstract interpretation.

This step is the bridge between the literal and abstract: students try to identify the important similes and metaphors in the poem, particularly if there is one central metaphor driving the entire piece. They should underline words or images they think might be focal points of an analysis. In this step, students should restrict themselves to identifying the metaphor itself rather than trying to interpret what it is representing.

Step 4: Abstract

Objective: Construct a thorough, cohesive interpretation that is supportable by the text.

Only once the language, action, and images are pinpointed can we consider the potential underlying meanings. In this step, emphasize to students that they need to get away from the concrete language used in the poem and to synthesize an interpretation that can be supported by evidence from the text.

Tip for Students: If the subject of your sentence is an image or word that is *in the poem*, you're still operating on the literal level. Make the subject of your sentence a feeling or idea that you think an image or word in the poem is trying to convey.

The four-step process is simple, but its simplicity is what makes it work so well. Easy to remember, easy to use. Suddenly, poems don't seem so insurmountable to the students.

A Creative Environment

What It Means and How to Get It

To achieve a truly creative environment, a teacher must create a safe space in the classroom. First, one of the tenets of forming any creative environment (whether classroom or workplace) is that there must be room for failure. No one is going to go out on a limb if they fear a misstep will result in criticism or ridicule (or getting fired, when it comes to an adult job). This is going to be scary territory for most students, no matter how methodical and disciplined an approach, so a teacher needs to address any reactions from other classmates that might disrupt or quash students' attempts. Even if students are going astray, wandering much too far from the actual text, consider what in their own experiences may be steering them in that direction.

While students are being asked to take the leap from literal to abstract, to create some kind of coherent interpretations of the lines in front of them, a teacher should repeatedly emphasize—for the benefit of the individual student as well as the class as a whole—that prior life experiences create "filters" for each of us; and because of these filters, individuals often will have different experiences (and interpretations) of the same subject or event. Just as important, we should keep in mind throughout this program that critical thinking and the interpretation of poetry require us to recognize our biases and proclivities and step back from them; indeed, poetry challenges us to step into the experience of the poem's speaker. There is a fine (but definitive) line between allowing creative license and setting up a free-for-all.

DEVELOPING A SKILL FOR RESPECTFUL DISCOURSE

Particularly in the last twenty-five years or so, we have been challenged by an extreme, polarized political climate. This means that the younger generations have never known anything different than this; furthermore, with the increased presence of editorial news on the television and the Internet, what is easily getting lost is the lesson of democracy as a "forum of ideas." The ideal environment envisioned by our forefathers does not mean that discussions based on individual convictions will not get heated, because that would be unrealistically and historically inaccurate. Going all the way back to the American Revolution, political discourse has been messy.

However, what students do need to learn is the value of listening, rather than immediately thinking of their next cutting, witty comeback—to the extent that they are not even hearing the other side they will ultimately respond to; they need to be less reactive and more proactive in their own thoughts, words, and actions. They need to respect that a differing view is not a threat, and not "less than" their own viewpoint.

By the same token, students will come to understand that a differing view or opinion is not trying to undermine their own or, even worse, undermine them as persons. And, with that understanding, they will not feel the need to immediately be on the defensive. We will continue to develop this sensibility in students throughout the program, building on it in the second half of the program when the classroom takes on a workshop environment.

SETTING UP THE CLASSROOM ENVIRONMENT

A teacher needs to facilitate a discussion by asking appropriate questions, questions that will push the students to go deeper into the text. If teachers find themselves doing more talking than asking, they would be wise to remind themselves that this context requires a focus on listening and then helping students piece together what they are coming up with on their own. Though the final interpretation at times may still have some wrinkles or ideas left untouched, it is ultimately a greater accomplishment than if the teacher has all but handed the students a specific, flawlessly articulated interpretation.

Teachers face particular challenges when facilitating classroom discussions of poetry. Because of poetry's more abstract nature compared to other forms of literature, it is easier for students to read into poems their own life experiences, for better or worse. For this reason, the teacher must be especially sensitive about the makeup of a class. Even when teaching multiple sections of a course during any given school day, the discussions of the same poem likely will go in quite different directions based on the makeup of that particular group of students. Consider the following points.

What is the class size?

Any teacher already is well aware of how a class size impacts the classroom dynamics, especially for discussions. In this context, the classroom size may determine how frequently the teacher wants to break up into smaller groups. A smaller group size may feel less intimidating for students who, especially at first, may be shy about suggesting possible interpretations of poetry. However, if a teacher does decide to use small-group work, it will be important to bring the small groups back together for a larger discussion: this will enable students to better see and appreciate the range of ideas and perspectives that their own classmates have generated.

Also, a teacher's role will likely shift in classes of different sizes. In small-group work, a teacher will have to manage several conversations at once—not just content, but also process—in other words, keeping the students grounded in the text, but also noting which students are taking on identifiable roles within the group. In this context, a teacher should at least identify the following as they emerge from a group:

- Leader: will drive a specific vision or set of ideas, prompting others to generate their own contributions.
- Coordinator: different than the leader; focused on the process of individuals working together through any suggested ideas.
- Recorder: writing down.
- "Finisher": catches the details, making sure the ideas make sense as a whole—will note any errors or weaknesses that need to be corrected for completion.

Is the class co-ed or all boys or girls?

At this age, students are becoming self-conscious, especially around members of the opposite sex. In single-sex environments, conversations not only may be less guarded, but the topics also may gravitate to less stereotypical areas. In a co-ed discussion, a teacher will want to help students avoid gender pitfalls in subject matter; she or he also will want to be attentive to the participation of each group, ensuring that neither the girls nor the boys are letting the other half dominate the discussion.

If co-ed, what is the ratio of boys to girls? Again, it will be easy for one group to identify the other as "other" and either try to dominate or relinquish control of the discussion. Especially in classes where one group substantially outnumbers the other, it will be easy for the smaller group to feel overwhelmed, vulnerable, and/or that the larger group has a perspective that matters more.

What is the ethnic/racial makeup of the class? What are the ratios of any identifiable groups in the class?

Having a diverse classroom is ideal for bringing in a range of ideas to any discussion. However, a teacher needs to make sure that any diverse perspective is given equal respect as well as equal time. Remembering that an integral part of this poetry program is to develop students' appreciation that multiple perspectives exist and each is valuable, how a class discussion goes is paramount.

Particularly during any exploration of diverse voices in poetry, a teacher must be ready for a discussion that may trigger some very interesting, perhaps even controversial, views. In this context, it will be important for a teacher to not give extra weight to any single perspective simply because it comes from a student who shares a commonality with the speaker of the poem.

For example, it would be a disservice to an African American student as much as to others in the class when interpreting Gwendolyn Brooks's poem "We Real Cool" to give his interpretation more weight simply because he also is African American. Besides being unfounded, this kind of treatment reinforces a sense of separation and separate experiences and lays the groundwork for students to make assumptions based on race or some other characteristic in the future—the antithesis of the goal here!

For the same reason, a teacher should be conscious of ratios among other possible self-identifying groups in a class. There is a concept in team building known as "fault lines": simply put, like geographic fault lines, these lie latent most of the time; but when activated they can cause seismic shifts. In teams or classes, all kinds of potential fault lines are right there beneath the surface and might be triggered depending on the task at hand.

For example, if a poem has as its subject matter woman's suffrage, a gender fault line likely will be triggered, and a teacher will have to ensure that the conversation stays inclusive and does not reduce itself to male/female binary interpretations. Another example: the speaker of a poem expresses an urban voice, perhaps with dialect indicating a lower education or socio-economic level; take care to ensure that the class does not inadvertently divide itself between the have and have-nots in the room.

Is this activity part of the core curriculum or part of an enrichment program? Or an extracurricular activity?

Where the poetry program is situated in a student's day-to-day is likely to figure heavily into how much effort and enthusiasm he or she brings to it. If the program is part of a core curriculum, it automatically gets validated as something "important" and something that gets a priority among other homework or scheduled commitments.

As an enrichment program within the school day, the program will get some attention, but teachers need to be sensitive to what else is on a student's plate: when assigning students to craft a poem for the next day when they have a couple of quizzes or a project due, expect the poems to be more hastily crafted (perhaps with the exception of a few who will use the poetry assignment to procrastinate studying for that science quiz!).

If the poetry program is simply an after-school program, any time working on poems at home is going to be happening after everything else, academic or otherwise, they have going on. In this case, a teacher is best advised to incorporate a very generous amount of in-classroom writing time, in addition to the integral class discussion time.

Is this part of a "gifted" program where students are high achievers?

Often, programs and activities that are about tapping into a child's creativity are made available to those who have scored well on standardized tests and/ or have a history of achieving top grades. A teacher, understandably, will get excited at the prospect of teaching a handful of hand-picked students whose promise matches their work ethic. Ah, the possibilities! However, if the students in a particular class have been gathered together using such criteria, teachers need to keep in mind that those who are good test takers or get high marks on their report cards may not always be the best budding poets.

An important tenet of this book is that each person, every student, has a unique perspective and, therefore, equal importance. And those who have earned the best grades in the past may not be the most comfortable with a less certain terrain. And the "stellar" students absolutely do not have an exclusive on the ability to come up with a great metaphor or image. In fact, students who have not done quite as well on other kinds of tasks may thrive on poetic grounds. So, while using poetry to help explore and foster creativity and encouraging students to keep open minds, teachers need to keep open minds as well: it's not unlikely that your Keats-in-disguise will show up in a student who has been keeping a low profile until now.

Is this part of a program for "troubled" or challenged students who have been identified as having special developmental or emotional needs?

The other side of the same coin: what if a teacher finds him- or herself in a room with students handpicked precisely because they have a history of academic or behavioral issues? Without weighing any kind of label too heavily, it is important to recognize—especially if there is any hope of collaborative work—the initial limitations a certain context presents. While this poetry program is designed in part to develop students' ability for respectful discourse, a teacher might anticipate greater resistance from students who have a history of acting out, not getting along with their peers, or have exhibited greater concern for "saving face" and keeping their guard up.

A suggestion for teachers in this kind of environment: be patient and understand that progress, even measured in baby steps, is still progress. Keeping to a structure and insisting on ground rules for any discussion will be key in maintaining order in the classroom as well as achieving the program's objectives.

What is the physical environment of the classroom like: are the students sitting at desks, in a circle, around a large table, and so forth?

In the last couple of decades, even in the adult workplace, the idea of a prestigious corner office has mostly gone by the wayside. These days, it's an open space, something to foster a creative flow. Even where individuals still have their own desks (or cubicles or four walls), companies are creating more common areas or using community collaborative spaces if their own cannot be reshaped. So what about the traditional classroom of individual desks in rows?

An egalitarian teacher will at least rotate the places, so no student is consistently relegated to the back, right? If the class size and classroom size can accommodate, however, taking the few minutes to move desks into a circle is worth the class period time to ensure that everyone feels like a part of the conversation.

And, as tough as it may be to get into the practice of it, among the teacher's challenges for facilitating discussion will be tracking to some extent the comments to make sure that each student is heard. Ideally, each student will contribute at least once each period. This can be done with a little prompting. It can be helpful for a teacher to keep a daily log and, at the end of each class period or session, simply go through the student roster to note any particularly strong insights, and also anyone who did not participate.

A good rule of thumb: don't let two classes go by with a student not contributing to the discussion. Try prompting the subsequent class; if still reticent, a gentle inquiry after class about what is happening can help a teacher remedy the problem. (Ill-prepared? Upset about something else going on at school or at home? Insecure about talking about poetry?) Sometimes students need a little extra assurance before they will readily plunge in.

Is this happening in a private or public school? A library or community center? Some other kind of institution?

This particular program has had success in a wide range of settings: public, private, or parochial schools; middle school, high school, after-school community centers; and even a juvenile detention institution. As one might expect, the tone of the class will reflect the larger environment.

Beyond the immediate atmosphere, there are additional considerations such as the kinds of resources a teacher might have access to. For example, in an elite private school, a teacher will have more resources at her or his disposal, including the ability to use a wide variety of books, including anthologies or shorter volumes of poetry by a specific poet. A public school teacher, on the other hand, may be limited to a particular textbook with the potential to supplement as much as one's Xerox budget allows.

Are the students part of this program by choice?

As with any activity, if a student is participating because it is a part of the regular, required curriculum, a teacher should expect a normal range of responses to the challenges that reading and writing poetry presents, whereas in an extra-curricular activity (unless a parent has made the decision for the student), a teacher will encounter more enthusiasm from participants. But the bulk of the students we are focused on here will, in fact, be studying poetry as part of a curriculum that has been handed to them, so what can a teacher do to offset this possible glitch? A simple approach to keep in mind is that, when at all possible, give the students a chance to make choices. Especially at the middle school and high school levels, students are just beginning to more actively assert their independence. What good is appreciating others' voices if they feel as though their own is not heard or respected?

So, while keeping it clear that she or he is in charge, a teacher can take care of the macro-organization of things and let the students make some micro-level decisions. For instance, it's easy enough for a teacher to present the students with a few poems rather than just a single poem that all can effectively serve the purpose of familiarizing students with the concept of personification. Why not offer up those poems and let the student decide which one he or she would like to develop an interpretation? Again, we want to nurture in the students an appreciation for diverse voices and an understanding that each person's voice counts. Let the student experience first-hand what it feels like to be valued, and it will be more impactful than anything you tell them about why respect matters.

What are the socio-economic backgrounds of your students? How disparate?

A teacher will need to consider resources—this time, not just what resources are at her or his disposal, but also what resources students might have at their disposal. Do they have laptops? Do they have Internet access at home? These circumstances will not only affect how comfortable and fluid they are at researching, writing, and putting together any polished presentation, but also will factor into the kinds of conversations they might be having in their homelife. Is the family sitting around the dinner table talking about the aspects of each family member's day? Will the students have the opportunity to share their ideas with family members and listen to theirs in a respectful environment? Is there intellectual curiosity and articulateness at home? Or do their situations not give them access to thoughtful conversations with adults (or siblings) at home? Is the student getting reinforcement (or resistance) from home that poetry matters?

A teacher needs to be especially sensitive to any disparity in resources when evaluating completed projects. While an objective rubric is indispensable in terms of fairness, a handwritten poster should not necessarily be counted as less than a more polished poster complete with printed-out impressive graphics. In fact, as we all know, like other DIY efforts, these might actually have required more time and energy to put together.

Is a student's participation specifically graded?

Participation is right at the backbone of any grading rubric in a program like this because it's the easiest, though not completely fail-safe, way of creating a level playing field. It's also a clear incentive for students, especially as an incentive to step outside one's own comfort zone. As noted, however, for one reason or another that should not be so quickly dismissed, some students may be reticent to speak up in class discussions or stretch themselves when it comes time to pen their own poems. Rather than penalizing students for this, a teacher should think about ways to reward students when they do finally make that leap.

But weighing participation heavily cuts both ways: a teacher will quickly identify if there is a student who is participating simply to get the check mark, quick to remark without putting much thought into what he or she is saying. So it is important that a teacher define participation thoroughly: thoughtful comments, genuine effort to further the discussion or offer a particular idea that can be anchored in the text.

Understand that students will fumble, and sometimes they will make a comment that is more than just a little rough around the edges; but these kinds of genuine contributions are completely different from speaking for the sake of speaking. The teacher's job will be, in part, to distinguish between these—specifically to teach the larger lesson of holding people accountable for what they say in a group context.

An Initial Classroom Activity

The Appointment Book

Beyond learning to collaborate, students need from an early age to work with a variety of people—not just their best buddies. And on the other side of the small-group-work coin: teachers need to ensure that the less popular students don't always find themselves in the awkward position of scrambling to find someone who will work with them. An easy way to address both of these concerns is by starting out the school year with a simple activity that helps set the tone and keep things organized throughout the year. In the "Appointment Book" activity, each student is handed a simple worksheet that looks as if it came straight out of a daily appointments book.

With their individual sheets in hand, students are given the time to walk around the room booking appointments with each other—a different person for each hour, 6:00 A.M. to 6:00 P.M.; totaling twelve separate appointments, twelve different classmates. This exercise invariably gets students mixing with students they would not necessarily work with otherwise. A bonus to using this method as a way of setting up future working partners: the typically less popular picks will, perhaps for the first time, experience what it feels like to be sought after! Toward the end of the activity when appointment hours are mostly full, a teacher may have to allow some students a second hour slot when they will work together; and, in these cases, it's best to encourage a group of three so that the experience is still a little different for each of them.

Once the hour time slots are filled up, require students to keep their individual appointment sheet in their binder or notebook to bring with them each day to class. Teachers would be wise to collect and copy the sheets in order to keep a "master set" handy, in case any are forgotten (or lost). Worth mentioning: if necessary, it's also possible to recover from a lost sheet by gathering information via a student's hourly counterparts.

13

So, what does the Appointment Book look like in practice? A teacher just has to announce which hour's appointment students should meet with for a given activity: "OK, class—everyone, get together with your three o'clock!" Keeping track of which hours are being selected will help a teacher ensure she or he is mixing it up enough. And, from time to time, it is not a bad idea to let students decide the appointment hour the class will be using that day: decision-making, even when it is something as simple as choosing an hour on a clock and therefore who they will be working with, can be empowering. And that's something we all can appreciate.

Lesson 1

Becoming an Active Reader

Even before you introduce students to the Four-Step Method for approaching and interpreting poems, assign "What Good Poems Are For" by Tom Wayman: students should read the poem and, in their notebooks, write five to six sentences about how, *in the poem* (making sure students understand the importance of always keeping their interpretations grounded in the text itself), poems are compared to plants.

What Good Poems Are For
To sit on a shelf in the cabin across the lake
where the young man and young woman
have come to live—there are only a few books
in this dwelling, and one of them
is this book of poems.

To be like plants
on a sunlit windowsill
of a city apartment—all the hours of care
that go into them, he tendering and watering,
and yet to the casual eye they are just present
—only a brief moment of enjoyment.
Only those who work on the plant
know how slowly it grows
and changes, almost dies from its own causes
or neglect, or how other plants
can be started from this one
and used elsewhere in the house
or given to friends.
But everyone notices the absence of plants

in a residence
even those who don't have plants for themselves.

There is also (this is more rare)
Bob Smith's story about the man in the bar up north,
a man in his 50's, taking a poem from a new book Bob showed him
around from table to table, reading it aloud
to each group of drinkers because, he kept saying,
the poem was about the work he did, what he knew about,
written by somebody like himself.
But where could he take it
except from table to able, past the
[. . .] *Hey that's pretty good?* Over the noise
of the jukebox and the bar's TV,
past the silence of the lake,
a person is speaking
in a world full of people are talking.
Out of all that is said, these particular words
put down roots in someone's mind
so that he or she likes to have them here—
these words no one was paid to write
that live with us for a while
in a small container
on the ledge where the light enters

A BRIEF ANALYSIS

Poems, like plants:

1. Grow, change, die, give rise to new poems or ideas and stories (as plants can be used to grow new plants)
2. Some people spend a great deal of time tending to them, while others just enjoy them for a moment, as diversion or decoration.
3. Even people who might not seem to care would notice if poems weren't there, just as people would likely notice any barren space that is absent of plants.

The most important aspect of this analogy is that it inevitably generates a discussion about poetry as a living art form. "Only those who work on a plant / know how slowly it grows" (lines 12–13). What is the relationship of the poet to his poem? Perhaps an even more important question: what is the relationship of the reader to a poem?

Giving rise to these questions, Wayman's poem is the perfect introductory piece because it puts the students to task. It empowers them, makes them see more clearly their role in the creative process. It helps them understand that the process is ongoing, and therefore whatever a poet creates by writing something down is just a seedling for the possibility of a variety of plants. *Light* is a metaphor for meaning, revelation, goodness—this metaphor, even the younger, middle school-age students will recognize as having been seen before in books as well as films and television programs. In this poem, the light that enters the window becomes a spectrum of possibilities. The prism is the poem itself. As if to underscore this point, the poem finishes without actually ending: the lack of a period implies the ongoing nature of the process, the regenerative nature of a poem.

In addition, the third stanza of this poem, with an eager bar goer trying with great enthusiasm to pass onto others a poem he relates to (lines 26–27), suggests the emotional rewards a poem can offer. More than a riddle that appeals to our intellect only, a poem can express an experience or viewpoint that also appeals to our individual nature. In this way, students can be drawn into poetry as they discover how it can validate their own emotions; and, they will see the possibility of expressing their own ideas and emotions through poetic form. Thus, Wayman's poem serves as the perfect launching pad for meaningful study and an increase in our awareness of the world around us, and our part in tending to that environment.

Lesson 2

Understanding the Central Metaphor

Although students are quick to pick out similes, sometimes metaphors can be a little more elusive. For this reason, it is easiest to start out with a poem like Robert Frost's "Mending Wall," which relies on one central image to make its point. Also, the language is straightforward and simple to follow, so a student's challenge is not compounded by a heap of new vocabulary words or perplexing phrasing.

Furthermore, because the title of the poem announces what the central metaphor will be, it becomes a good illustration of how a poem's title sometimes can be extremely helpful as a quick first clue as to what's in store. It is a good practice to get into to immediately take note of a title and ask oneself (or the class) what, if any, things it might convey. What expectations might it be setting up for the reader? And, to bring a student's interpretive process full circle, a teacher can foster the habit of revisiting a title as a final consideration once all the steps have been worked through and the process is nearly complete.

Mending Wall

Something there is that doesn't love a wall,
That sends the frozen-ground-swell under it,
And spills the upper boulders in the sun;
And makes gaps even two can pass abreast.
The work of hunters is another thing:
I have come after them and have made repair
Where they have left not one stone on a stone,
But they would have the rabbit out of hiding,
To please the yelping dogs. The gaps I mean,
No one has seen them made or heard them made,
But at spring mending-time we find them there.
I let my neighbor know beyond the hill;

And on a day we meet to walk the line
And set the wall between us once again.
We keep the wall between us as we go.
To each the boulders that have fallen to each.
And some are loaves and some so nearly balls
We have to use a spell to make them balance:
"Stay where you are until our backs are turned!"
We hear our fingers rough with handling them.
Oh, just another kind of outdoor game,
One on a side. It comes to little more:
He is all pine and I am apple orchard.
My apple trees will never get across
And eat the cones under his pines, I tell him.
He only says, "Good fences make good neighbors."
Spring is the mischief in me, and I wonder
If I could put a notion in his head:
"Why do they make good neighbors? Isn't it
Where there are cows? But there are no cows.
Before I built a wall I'd ask to know
What I was walling in or walling out,
And to whom I was like to give offense.
Something there is that doesn't love a wall,
That wants it down." I could say "Elves" to him,
But it's not elves exactly, and I'd rather
He said it for himself. I see him there
Bringing a stone grasped firmly by the top
In each hand, like an old-stone savage armed.
He moves in darkness as it seems to me,
not of woods only and the shade of trees.
He will not go behind his father's saying,
And he likes having thought of it so well
he says again, "Good fences make good neighbors."

FOUR STEPS: MENDING WALL

Step 1: Vocabulary

New Vocabulary Words—the language in this poem is relatively simple; there should not be any words that are uncertain to the average middle school student.

Step 2: Literal

This is one poem that works particularly well with role-playing because it is so easy to visualize. Create a boundary using a row of desks, or the like; one student to the left, one to the right. Then let the students recreate the conversation contained within the poem in their own words (paraphrasing!). Although this poem is not broken into stanzas, it does follow grammatical rules in terms of sentence structure. It is fairly easy, therefore, to break down by sentences and ideas. Try to paraphrase every five lines or so and have students write down these summaries in their notebooks.

Step 3: Figurative Language

Identify the central metaphor of the poem as *the wall* or *fence*.

Step 4: Abstract

Take each idea written down as part of the paraphrasing process and then try to extend it into more universal ideas, not limited to the circumstances of the poem. If the central metaphor is the wall, what does the wall represent?

ASSIGNMENT

Write a paragraph (five to seven sentences) explaining why good fences make good neighbors.

In trying to generate ideas that will create a well-developed paragraph, students inevitably will wind up writing ideas that are on a more abstract level. Most likely, the paragraphs will talk about boundaries, the sense of personal space and property, and individual versus collective ownership.

A discussion of individual ownership, perhaps with a little guidance, could turn into a discussion of how ownership affects self-identity. Especially at the middle school and high school levels, as students are beginning to develop a greater sense of self, by shifting the focus of discussion toward something more personally relevant yet still clearly grounded in the text, a teacher can illustrate how poetry is a creative art form to be approached mindfully and meticulously, and also an art form that is malleable and open for myriad interpretations.

Following the initial assignment and a full discussion during which students share their work, a teacher should ask students to write a second paragraph specifically about lines 31 and 32: "Before I built a wall I'd ask to know / What I was walling in or walling out." Use this exercise to highlight how we (writer or reader) can take one image—in this case, a wall—and use it in multiple, sometimes surprising, ways. Here, the wall not only is protective by enclosing one's things and protecting them from anything "outside" that is bad, but it also can possibly shut out the *good* things. A teacher can suggest that this "flip side" to exclusion might also be extended to our un-derstanding of how narrow-mindedness might shut out our ability to let in other people's viewpoints: we could be doing ourselves a great disservice by discounting ideas, people, or things just because they are different from what we are used to.

Remember this is the starting point for students, so it is better to let them absorb a few points rather than trying to get them to dissect the poem into oblivion. What is most important in this lesson is that students start to gain confidence in their ability to recognize a metaphor; and that they come away with an understanding that, even within a single poem, the same metaphor can communicate different ideas.

Some students may take to the active interpretation process as soon as the first lesson; others may take much more time. The role of a teacher, then, is to facilitate whatever progress, as it comes naturally; all the while, she or he should keep in mind that it is developing the ability to work through a process of interpretation—rather than acquiring knowledge or details of a specific poem—that is our goal.

THE BIGGER PICTURE

Along with taking these first steps in the interpretive process using the Frost poem as a vehicle, students will be starting to formulate ideas about bound-aries and inclusion that should facilitate good initial discussions concerning what others might (or might not) be able to contribute to our own individual-ized experiences.

Lesson 3

Literary Terms and Devices

IRONY

It is important from the onset of any poetry program to emphasize that extracting a nonliteral meaning is the main objective of using the delineated four-step method and any subsequent discussions or other interpretative exercises. And the goal of getting beyond the literal is one a teacher will have to repeat and reinforce again and again throughout the program. In order to get past the literal, however, students must develop their interpretive skills and be able to effectively argue their assertions with support from the text; they must learn the vocabulary of analysis, including the variety of devices employed by poets. Students need to recognize the basic building blocks such as irony, personification, and so forth, as well as stylistic choices such as alliteration and dialect.

Before offering a textbook definition of irony, let the students read together Theodore Roethke's "My Papa's Waltz."

My Papa's Waltz
The whiskey on your breath
could make a small man dizzy;
But I hung on like death:
Such waltzing was not easy.

We romped until the pans
Slid from the kitchen's shelf;
My mother's countenance
Could not unfrown itself.

The hand that held my wrist
Was battered on one knuckle;

At every step you missed
My right ear scraped a buckle.

You beat time on my head
With a palm caked hard by dirt
Then waltzed me off to bed
Still clinging to your shirt.

FOUR STEPS: MY PAPA'S WALTZ

Step 1: Vocabulary

Simple language is used, but it may be helpful to look up *waltz* to determine the exact nature of the dance. (In addition to looking up *waltz* in a dictionary, a teacher should pull up some video examples of a waltz.)

Step 2: Literal

Father and child are dancing around the kitchen as mother looks on.

- *Who is the speaker?* Is it a child, or an adult looking back through the eyes of a child? Boy or girl? Does the identity of the speaker change the effect of the poem?

Step 3: Figurative Language

Possible metaphor—the dance between the parent and child

Step 4: Abstract

The dance serves as a metaphor for the whole parent-child relationship: a struggle, mixed with love. Although the child is being hurt (the parent is all too human), he lets the father carry him off to bed, "still clinging to his shirt." This dance thus conveys the sense of attachment involved in such a relationship, as well as themes of unconditional love and forgiveness.

A BRIEF ANALYSIS AND THE BIGGER PICTURE

This is a tough poem to read because of the undercurrent of violence present in the scene. However, it is one of the poems students most unanimously respond to immediately with enthusiasm. Because all of the students have experienced some kind of struggle with their parents (though hopefully not as extreme), they readily relate to what is happening here in the kitchen.

Moreover, when students find that they relate to a poem, as in this case, without having ever been subjected themselves to this specific kind of brutal handling, they quickly grasp with this poem how finding relevance *requires* transcending the literal.

Beyond this, students typically pick up on the idea that, although this is a rough scene and the relationship between father and child is unsettling (compounded by the troubling presence of a mother who looks on disapprovingly, but passively), there is still a sense of love. Particularly for students at this age, the love and desire for approval expressed through the metaphor of the clumsy waltz surely will resonate.

Students at this age also often respond to the portrayal of parents as less than ideal—indeed, this is the age when many students are beginning to see their own parents in a more realistic, less idealized light: parents cannot always make things better; parents can mess up; parents are human, too, and therefore deserving of our compassion as well.

So, without an elablorate introduction to the concept of irony, a teacher can simply invite students into the world of this dance. A jolly dance around the kitchen—hardly jolly, as it turns out. A teacher just needs to explain that this poem uses irony without handing the class a pat definition; students likely will be able to surmise the meaning of the term on their own. Most already will be familiar with the common throwaway, "Isn't it ironic?" Although this idiomatic phrase is not quite correct in its use of the term, it tends to be enough to lead students in the right direction. Students will grasp the meaning of *irony* without anyone's having to write a definition on the board.

One more aspect of this poem that proves useful, especially at this juncture, is its use of rhyme. It has already been suggested that a teacher refrain from assigning poems employing end rhymes, at least until the very end of the program when students have a deeper appreciation for figurative language as the core of the poetic form. Poems heavy on rhyme, if presented too early on in the program, will only reinforce students' preconceived notions about what makes a poem a poem (synonymous, unfortunately all too often, with *rhyme*).

However, here's an example of the use of rhyme at its best: Roethke's simple structure and rhyme here underscore the lightness of the dance, the easy rhythm of the dance—in turn, making the irony presented in the unsteady, fumbling dance happening in the poem all the more pronounced.

THE BIGGER PICTURE

How does this poem fit in with our agenda in terms of developing awareness? In addition to its arguably sympathetic view of the parents, the poem primarily gets students to take a closer look at something familiar and acknowledge that things may be a bit more complicated than what appears at first glance. While the poem on a superficial, quick-read level might seem jovial enough, it becomes very clear that this is absolutely *not* a picture of the perfect family.

Students might start thinking about how they tend to make assumptions about other people they know—perhaps even classmates—and can be too quick to judge. Also, this poem illuminates affection that embraces (literally, in the case of the child and father dancing) imperfection. Thus, being able to appreciate certain elements of someone and even have some kind of relationship with him or her does not preclude recognizing and struggling with the flaws that come with that person.

Appreciating diversity does not mean ignoring differences, including points of conflict; rather, the appreciation is about finding what beauty is there, despite the rough edges.

Another poem that works well in this lesson, particularly as a follow-up to Roethke's poem, is Stevie Smith's "Not Waving but Drowning":

Not Waving but Drowning
Nobody heard him, the dead man,
But still he lay moaning:
I was much further out than you thought
And not waving but drowning.

Poor chap, he always loved larking
And now he's dead
It must have been too cold for him his heart gave way,
They said.

Oh, no, no, no, it was too cold always
(Still the dead one lay moaning)
I was much too far out all my life
And not waving but drowning.

FOUR STEPS: NOT WAVING BUT DROWNING

Step 1: Vocabulary

New Vocabulary Words—larking

Larking is a slang term, whose meaning can be derived through context easily enough. However, a teacher should get students into the habit of reaching for the dictionary. Although being able to ascertain meaning through context is a necessary skill, it should not be relied upon as heavily in poetry because the text can be more ambiguous than it generally is in works of prose, and also because the nuance of a definition can make all the difference.

For example, while the words *pacing* and *strolling* both connote movement and a kind of walking, clearly these two words convey something entirely different from each other; naturally, a student would want to understand the difference between these two words if he or she encountered one or both in a poem.

Step 2: Literal

Someone is out in the water (ocean or lake); people on the shore think the person is waving to them, when actually he is trying to signal to them that he is drowning. No one understands, and so no one helps. In the poem, the people and the dead man both seem to be remembering this episode after the fact.

- *Who is the speaker?* The poem is a terrific example of how a speaker can change within a poem. The first stanza is an omniscient narrator of sorts; in the second stanza, the speaker is the collective voice of the people who were witnesses to the man's waving; the third stanza's speaker is the man drowning.

More on Stanza Formation

Discussion of the changes in speaker in Smith's poem also can lead into a discussion about stanza formation. While the line breaks may seem unusual (very varied in length, no end rhymes), students should be able to see how each stanza shifts, like a paragraph: a new stanza is used when the speaker, and therefore the perspective, changes.

In addition, the third stanza is the perspective of the dead man who "still . . . lay moaning." How can he be dead and yet still, apparently, alive? A class discussion might touch on how living an empty or lonely life can make one dead in spirit, living without hope, simply going through the motions of day-to-day life. This interpretation would seem to fit with the description of the man in this poem, and also signal a move away from interpreting this poem to be about a literal (corporeal) death.

Step 3: Figurative Language

Possible metaphor—swimming, drowning

Step 4: Abstract

The drowning and being "too far out" suggests the man's alienation and inability to communicate with others. It also suggests tendencies to misinterpret, misunderstand, or simply not notice the truth about a person or situation. Some students may bring up the theme of appearance versus reality—and, if they have not yet been introduced to this common theme in literature, this lesson would be an opportune time for a teacher to do so.

Another opportunity provided by this poem is a quick focus on word choice: a teacher should take time during this lesson to point out the use of the word *further*. As a general rule, *farther* is used to communicate distance, whereas *further* is reserved for implying an additional something. So, did the poet use this word purposely? Let the students play with the use of *further*, to see if its use, if defined as "additional," perhaps alters the meaning of the line at all. Again, emphasis is on the necessity of precision in language, especially for an art form that relies on condensed language.

"My Papa's Waltz" and "Not Waving but Drowning" work well together. Both rely on the disparity between what seems to be happening and what is actually happening (irony). By letting the students wade through the poems before explaining the term, they will discover the meaning of irony and its usefulness for themselves.

THE BIGGER PICTURE

The Stevie Smith poem, like "My Papa's Waltz," makes the point to its readers that what we see at a glance may not be what is happening at all. A teacher can extend the discussion to focus on the broader topics of communication and miscommunication in general. A challenge that comes out of the existence of multiple perspectives is that much of what we try to convey to each other might be misinterpreted or lost altogether. In the case of the Smith poem, this miscommunication or failure to connect becomes a matter of life and death.

How then, can we work toward minimizing the misconstrued words and events in our own interactions and maximize our ability to share experiences and exchange ideas? Students may talk about how each individual brings with her- or himself, to any given situation, a set of preconceived notions; these notions are based on their unique background and past experiences, and they function as a kind of filter whenever communication is taking place, whether she or he is on the sending or receiving end.

What becomes increasingly apparent as a class discussion continues is the need for us all to be more sensitive to differences in our backgrounds and aware of how those differences might color any interactions among us. Once we understand this, we are challenged to work harder at finding common ground, while at the same time never dismissing the differences—because, ultimately, we will want to take all aspects of all perspectives into account for the fullest, and often most rewarding, view.

TONE

A lesson about tone naturally follows from a discussion of irony. In this lesson, the poems demonstrate how, rather than subtleties of content implying a meaning that is different from the one most obvious, the *tone* of the poem can be the key to a poem's meaning. A discussion of tone also necessitates a further discussion of the identity—the voice—of the speaker—for example, the following William Carlos Williams poem.

This Is Just to Say
I have eaten
the plums
that were in
the icebox

and which
you were probably
saving
for breakfast

Forgive me
they were delicious
so sweet
and so cold

FOUR STEPS: THIS IS JUST TO SAY

Step 1: Vocabulary

As with other poems we have discussed so far, this poem is simple in its language, reinforcing the idea to students that poems are not necessarily about lofty words and recondite language. In fact, if you were to ask students what this poem sounds like, some almost assuredly will respond that it sounds like an ordinary note tacked onto a refrigerator door or left on a kitchen table.

Step 2: Literal

A person has eaten some plums left by another (relationship between the two people unknown), without asking first. The poem is written after the fact to inform and also, ostensibly, to apologize.

- *Who is the speaker?* The speaker is the person who has eaten the plums. Age, sex, or other characteristics of the speaker are not described, so we cannot be sure of his or her personality and, therefore, the sincerity of the note.

- Next question: If this were an actual note left for someone to read, imagine what the handwriting would be like. Is it careful, deliberate, or scribbled down quickly as an after-thought?

How students decide to answer this question might lead them to envision the speaker in a certain way or with a particular disposition; and this image could, in turn, significantly impact students' thoughts on the possible motivation for writing the note.

Step 3: Figurative Language

While this poem, in its simplicity, does not make use of obvious similes, metaphors, or other literary devices, in order for it to be a poem (as opposed to just a note) there must be a suggestion of something beyond what is most readily apparent in its language. It is something more than a note . . . but what? So a teacher's challenge here is to bring into focus the *situation* presented in the poem (like the dance in Roethke's "My Papa's Waltz") and suggest to students that it is this context and the broader implications it provides that earn the poem its status as artistic expression.

Step 4: Abstract

The situation in this poem reflects the experience of doing something we shouldn't do and feeling sorry or guilty afterward . . . *or* maybe just trying to get away with having done something we should not have done. The tone is what makes this poem interesting: as it comes across most clearly in the third stanza, the apologetic tone directly clashes with the speaker's not failing to mention how "so delicious" the plums were, despite the brevity of the overall message. Here, a teacher should point out, is a sharp signal to the reader that things are not as simple in this little poem as they might seem at first glance.

In fact, with this brief poem and lesson about tone, a teacher has a shining example of why it is good practice to always read a poem at least twice through. If you did not pick up on the tone the first time around, hopefully on the second time around some of a poem's more subtle but crucial aspects will become more apparent. Here, while the speaker asks for forgiveness, she or he, at the same time, reveals in tone an incongruence between words and meaning when she or he adds that the plums were "delicious / so sweet / and so cold." This description, if anything, seems to further the transgression, rubbing it in rather than attempting to soften the blow. It is this very last section of the poem, then, that separates it from something stuck on a refrigerator door with a magnet.

An alternative interpretation might be that the poem is suggesting the complexity, often self-conflicted nature, of human motivation; that, when people succumb to selfishness or indulge their desires or whims at the expense of others, they often become overwrought with guilt ex post facto. So the question then becomes whether this message is a genuine sign of remorse. Or is it merely a thinly disguised attempt to alleviate one's own guilt?

Conflicted emotions such as these likely will resonate with students this age particularly: at this age, they are still vulnerable to "getting in trouble" with authority figures in their lives (parents, teachers, coaches) when they fall short; but they also are becoming more self-aware and self-regulating, and so can relate to feeling guilty about doing something wrong even when they are not caught in the act and facing a reprimand.

Conversely, taking into account the tone of the poem, a reader might be compelled to counter the above interpretations with a slightly less sympathetic view: underneath the good manners and politeness, humans can be selfish and even downright nasty. The speaker eats the plums that are not his or hers; the message is left for the other person to find, conveniently after the fact. What's more, the apology comes in a way that makes sure the person addressed knows exactly what she or he missed out on.

The tone in this poem provides an added dimension, the complexity, that readers expect of a poem. Not only does it open the door for multiple interpreations, but interpretations that seem to say quite opposite things about human nature. In "This Is Just to Say," the tone rather than the images or word choices per se is what allows the poet to transform the ordinary into the poetic.

THE BIGGER PICTURE

A teacher can use this poem as a vehicle toward enhancing students' own interpersonal skills. Building on the more general topic of communication as it was first introduced during the lesson centered on the Roethke and Smith poems, a teacher should engage students in a discussion that elaborates on the effects tone can have on one's oral as well as written communication with others. As important as what we say is how we say it. Therefore, the class can "play" with a few sentences or lines from this poem by changing the emphasis or tone in their voices. In doing so, the class can discuss the impact these changes are likely to have on how the words would be received and interpreted.

As a final exercise before moving on to the next poem, teachers might assign students to create a message similar to the one in the Williams poem—but write it as a note, then as an e-mail, then as a text message or tweet. Discuss how each of these well-accepted short forms of everyday communications might have some pitfalls to watch out for, with the potential for a missed or misinterpreted tone at the top of the list.

We Real Cool
THE POOL PLAYERS.
SEVEN AT THE GOLDEN SHOVEL.

We real cool. We
Left school. We

Lurk late. We
Strike straight. We
Sing sin. We
thin gin. We

Jazz June. We
Die soon.

(Gwendolyn Brooks)

As in the Williams poem, the voice of the speaker(s) in this poem is clear and is more similar to speech one might hear in everyday life than it is to language emanating from an eloquent poet. At the same time, it is important to note that, while this is an extremely good example of the use of dialect (and will inevitably be associated with specific racial and cultural stereotypes, which the teacher needs to address), the language of this poem is clearly *not* intended to resemble speech used in everyday conversation—people do not go around speaking in truncated rhyming couplets!

Nevertheless, the rhyme pattern gives this poem a "catchy" beat that students typically pick up on immediately, making it an almost guaranteed instant favorite. Don't be surprised if students are walking around saying-singing these lines to themselves, and to each other, months after the class has tackled this poem.

FOUR STEPS: WE REAL COOL

Step 1: Vocabulary

New Vocabulary—*jazz* as a verb;[1] *thin gin* might require some explanation. Also, a teacher should seize the opportunity this poem provides to discuss the use of slang and how using slang can affect the overall tone of a poem. Furthermore, does the use of slang draw a reader in, or can it alienate the reader? If the use of language does in fact create a sense of "other" and alienate the reader, what kind of impact—negative or otherwise—might this have on a reader's interpretation of the poem?

Step 2: Literal

Seven pool players at a billiards hall or bar called The Golden Shovel are hanging out, commenting on their life, which seems to consist of little else besides playing pool.

- *Who is the speaker?* ("We") The pool players are talking here as they inform the reader they've left school and this is how they spend their days. In addition to how they describe their day-to-day routine, their slang confirms a lack of education or desire to deal with anything other than playing pool and drinking gin.

- *Who is the audience?* While we might say that the speakers of this poem are addressing us, who is the *us*?

   Assuming they are directly addressing the reader(s) is a good starting point, but not necessarily the only possibility. For example, perhaps they are addressing the authority figures in their own lives, the ones telling them they should be in school or that they should abide certain rules. In other words, the intended audience might be the establishment at large.

   Or, with so much emphasis on the "we" in this poem, the audience being addressed in this poem might be interpreted as all outsiders—namely, anyone other than the "we" pool players. This interpretation underscores the separation the speakers feel from the rest of the world beyond the pool hall.

Exploring the Speaker: An In-Class Assignment

Begin by asking students to visualize the players and briefly write down in their notebooks a description of what the players look like—whether they are boys or girls, what they are wearing, how old they are, and so forth. Next, read some of the students' descriptions aloud.

   A teacher should not be surprised when some gender bias emerges: the pool players are almost certainly going to be envisioned as boys; however, a range of responses when it comes to the age of the pool players and their race or ethnicity is not unlikely. Some students may picture boys close to their own age or slightly older, as teenagers; others might picture recent high school dropouts or boys nearing their twenties; still others might picture much older men who have been hanging around the pool hall for years, doing the same thing day after day and getting nowhere.

As far as the race or ethnicity of the speakers, some students might be quick to assume that the speakers are African American if they are at all familiar with Gwendolyn Brooks as an African American poet, and even more ready to make that leap if they are familiar with her other poems or her Chicago roots. A teacher needs to address any presumptions about race and insist students articulate exactly what language or image in the poem lends itself to their interpretation.

Step 3: Figurative Language

The use of slang could signal that, although they might be aware of proper words and grammar, they are deliberately choosing to ignore the rules in favor of their own way. Perhaps they are using an alternative language as a way of feeling like they belong: somehow this slang speech they share is part of how they are able to create their own little world contained within the walls of the Golden Shovel; it is a world in which they feel more in control of their lives while at the same time setting themselves apart from others.

Step 4: Abstract

While the poem begins "we real cool," the rest of the poem suggests that things are not as *all right* as the speakers would have us believe. How cognizant of this fact the speakers are themselves is unclear. However, the last lines ("We / Die soon") does indicate an acknowledgment on some level of the futility of their lives. The tone is slick, "cool"; yet, the seriousness of their dead-end lives—the paralysis—is at the core of the poem.

More On Line Breaks

The repetition and placement of the word *we* opens up the possibility for class discussion to include a poem's structure—specifically, its line breaks. Visually, it's nearly impossible to miss this element of the poem's construction and hard to dismiss it as anything other than deliberate placement to achieve a desired effect. So, what is the effect?

What will potentially come out of this discussion is an exploration of collective identity, or what many students may identify as typical gang mentality. Consider the comfort one gains in a sense of belonging; the necessity to feel like part of a larger group for emotional needs, as well as for protection in an urban environment; the old cliché that misery loves company; how being part of a crowd and being exposed to peer pressure can result in a person losing sense of their own individual identity; how this loss might impact someone's motivation and reshape their sense of purpose; how a gang or group of friends can replace family (notice there is no mention of family in this poem). These are just some of the topics that students tend to bring up over and over again in regard to this poem—issues they find, usually in some less extreme form, applicable to their own lives.

Shifting the focus from language and slang to tone (continue reinforcing previous lessons by returning to earlier concepts), a teacher should ask students to recall situations they have been in, or know of, where someone sounds "cool" and carefree—particularly around other friends—while in reality that person is grappling with underlying issues and fears. The students understand, then, that it is exactly this tone that makes the lives and situation depicted in this poem more revealing—and moving—to its readers.

THE BIGGER PICTURE

The poem of the pool players at The Golden Shovel is a golden opportunity to discuss racial and cultural stereotypes. A teacher can steer class discussion to explore the hazards of oversimplifying or overgeneralizing. Stereotypes are not unlike Frost's wall as they confine us in our own thinking, effectively shutting out many things that could be positives in our lives.

Through the in-class activity, students will have more time to reflect on tendencies to make broad assumptions based on just a few salient characteristics of a person. Most of the time, these assumptions happen without any intentional ill-will, but they can still be harmful. The judgments we make might turn out to be fairly accurate, or they might be completely off base; there's just no way to know for sure when we have based our view on so few facts.

Going back to the range of responses by students when asked to write down their own visual of Brooks's pool players will drive home the point that different people will draw different conclusions, even when they are given the same exact information. Which are closer to the truth? Which are faulty? Is any one "better" or more accurate than the other? There is no right answer here, as is often the case in life; we are all piecing things together in our own way. A key takeaway from this lesson, then, is that students understand each of us must approach this task of piecing together bits of experience *responsibly* and—just as important—be respectful of others who are doing the same.

OTHER TOOLS FOR THE TOOLBOX

After exploring the use of dialect and slang, and revisiting the power of tone in a poem, "We Real Cool" gives a teacher additional opportunities in terms of developing students' understanding of poetry construction: close this lesson with an introduction to the use of *alliteration*, *assonance*, and *internal rhyme*, well-illustrated in the poem.

NOTE

1. In addition to looking up a definition for *jazz*, students almost certainly will be nonplussed by what it means to *jazz June*. I was fortunate enough to attend an afternoon-long session with the late Ms. Brooks held in November 1996 at Chicago State University, during which a small group of teachers were given the opportunity to discuss several of her poems with her, including this one. Ms. Brooks explained that *June* in this context meant "the establishment."

A Classroom Test

While it is important for a teacher to encourage multiple perspectives, and so allow room for creative responses, she or he must not do so at the expense of developing a disciplined approach to poetry and a skill set for meaningful analyses. The following test design expects students to follow the four-step method they have been practicing and requires them to exhibit analytical skills including the recognition of literary devices and terms they have learned thus far. Note that the start of the test prompts the student to write out the four steps. Besides earning the graded points with this response, students will be able to use this first part as a reference for the remainder of the test, keeping them anchored and on track.

The following template may be used in whole or in part:

PART I:

Briefly describe the four steps we use to read a poem.

Step 1:

Step 2:

Step 3:

Step 4:

PART II:

    (A) Read the following poem by Robert Hayden and work through the four-step method to explain what is happening *literally* in the poem, then what themes and *emotions* the poet is expressing. Each step should be clearly identified and answered specifically, as we have done in class.

(B) Under the appropriate step, describe the poem's speaker.

(C) Provide a short paragraph about the poem's *tone*.

(D) In a well-developed paragraph (five to seven sentences), *compare* this poem to Theodore Roethke's "My Papa's Waltz," which we discussed in class.

Note: You may use your dictionary to look up any words you are uncertain of that are contained within the Hayden poem; you may use your marked up text (your class copy) of Roethke's poem.

Those Winter Sundays

Sundays too my father got up early
and put his clothes on in the blueblack cold,
then with cracked hands that ached
from labor in the weekday weather made
banked fires blaze. No one ever thanked him.

I'd wake and hear the cold splintering, breaking.
When the rooms were warm, he'd call,
and slowly I would rise and dress,
fearing the chronic angers of the house.

Speaking indifferently to him,
who had driven out the cold
and polished my good shoes as well.
What did I know, what did I know
of love's austere and lonely offices?

(Robert Hayden)

ROETHKE AND HAYDEN: ANALYSIS POINTS

Like Roethke's "My Papa's Waltz," Hayden's "Those Winter Sundays" explores the relationship between a father and child. The poem is written in the past tense; the speaker is an adult recollecting his or her childhood. Similarly to father and child in "My Papa's Waltz," the two in Hayden's poem are, at least in part, defined by their trouble in communicating their love for each other. Furthermore, there is a hint of violence or unrest ("the chronic angers of the house"), that is not entirely unlike the home environment depicted in Roethke's poem.

Comparing the speakers of these two poems, the child in "My Papa's Waltz," who clings to the father with an unconditional love and an underlying tenderness, seems quite a contrast to the child in Hayden's poem, who speaks "indifferently" toward the father. It would be unlikely for the father and child of Hayden's poem to be found romping around the room together. On a more positive note, the father in "Those Winter Sundays" is not a drunkard; the speaker tells us he is a hardworking—albeit, undemonstrative—man.

Thus, while both poems are about a child and father, they actually are quite different in what they are conveying about the parent-child relationship. A comparison of these two poems will highlight for students once again the difference between literal and figurative. Yes, both poems focus on a father and child, but the two poems reflect very different relationships.

The noticeable contrast extends to a discussion about the tone of these poems. While both poems are nostalgic, the additional details of "Those Winter Sundays" create a tone primarily of regret, as an adult speaker looks back on a childhood memory with a perspective now stripped of childhood's naivete. The speaker now understands the loneliness of the adult world and, more importantly, understands how the father's labors, in themselves, were expressions of love.

One of the primary reasons Hayden's poem is effective at this juncture is because of its ostensible similarities to "My Papa's Waltz." Although student comparisons of these poems will note some crucial differences, the poems are similar enough on the surface so that the Hayden poem, seen for the first time by the students when they take the test, will feel like somewhat familiar turf for them, which will bolster their confidence and also give weaker students something to grab ahold of, so that they do not feel totally adrift, and panic. In addition, it is good at this point in their study of poetry for students to begin to see recurring images and themes.

THE BIGGER PICTURE

A good test reinforces lessons learned while at the same time assessing a student's grasp of the material. But the best kind of test not only challenges students, but also leads to some new thinking. Hayden's poem, even more than Roethke's, explores the nuances of a relationship most students possess in their own lives. Each student has a parent or guardian in his life, and it can be beneficial for him to contemplate how he might view that person now versus how he might view that person years from now as an adult.

Perhaps the words of Hayden's speaker will resonate just enough to make these young students pause and reflect and absorb some wisdom beyond their years. Here, the unspoken lesson is about accepting the imperfection of our own perspective and about its capacity to change. It is a lesson about respect and, most of all, about communication.

Lesson 4

Personification

PERSONIFICATION

Because the word *person* is visible in this literary term, a teacher can start off this lesson by writing the word on the board and asking students to guess what it means to "person-ify" something. Once the class has made some suggestions (let them go into detail, perhaps coming up with some examples on their own), have them look up the word in their dictionaries. The teacher can then write a full definition on the board and have the class copy it down into their individual notebooks, where they should keep a running list of literary terms.

A teacher should supply each student with a copy of the following Emily Dickinson poem before reading it aloud. Because there are some difficult words in this one, it is better for the teacher to read this one first, as the students read along; this will enable them to concentrate more on *hearing* the poem and trying to process what is happening in it, rather than being too distracted by the few words that are puzzling to them.

> Because I could not stop for Death—
> He kindly stopped for me—
> The carriage held but just Ourselves—
> And Immortality.
>
> We slowly drove—He knew no haste
> And I had put away
> My labor and my leisure too,
> For His Civility—

We passed the school, where Children strove
At Recess—in the Ring—
We passed the Fields of Grazing Grain—
We passed the Setting Sun—

Or rather—He passed Us—
The Dews drew quivering and chill—
For only Gossamer, my Gown—
My Tippet—only Tulle—

We paused before a house that seemed
A Swelling of the Ground—
The Roof was scarcely visible—
The Cornice—in the Ground—

Since then—'tis Centuries—and yet
Feels shorter than the Day
I first surmised the Horses' Heads
Were toward eternity—

FOUR STEPS:
BECAUSE I COULD NOT STOP FOR DEATH—

Step 1: Vocabulary

New Vocabulary—leisure, gossamer, tippet, tulle, cornice, surmise

This poem offers the perfect opportunity to show students why they cannot settle for the first or most succinct definition they find. For example, it is important that they understand the definition of *tulle* specifically enough to understand that Dickinson is providing us with an image of a bride in this poem.

Similarly, they will need to know more about a cornice than that it is part of a building. They should know it is something that decorates a *rooftop* because this provides the reader with a sense of direction and moving upward; in the poem,the cornice appears to be "in the ground" because the carriage is rising away from the Earth. If the students' concept of a cornice is vague, this detail will be lost on them.

Step 2: Literal

With a poem of this length and structure, it is a good idea for the class to tackle it one stanza at a time; in doing so, a teacher will have the opportunity to reinforce the lesson that any kind of assertion—literal or abstract—should be supported by actual words in the text.

But remember, during this step a teacher is just trying to help students create a blueprint for themselves that will anchor them in the subsequent *Abstract* step. At its best, this step serves as a reference point—a "check" for themselves—to make sure any interpretation remains grounded in the text, that any assertions can be supported by words or images there on the page, and that any final interpretation is cohesive.

stanza one—The speaker, somewhat hurried ("I could not stop") is offered a ride by a carriage driver, who is characterized as kind and gentle.

stanza two—Unlike the speaker, the driver seems to be in no rush ("He knew no haste"); the speaker settles in for the ride.

stanza three—The carriage passes by everyday scenes of children playing, fields, and finally the setting sun.

stanza four—The speaker has the sensation that they are standing still and that things are passing them by instead; the speaker then describes what she is wearing.

stanza five—The carriage passes by a house (the perspective puts the speaker above the house).

stanza six—The speaker tells us that it has been centuries since this ride occurred, though it feels like it just happened ("Feels shorter than a day"). In the last two lines, the speaker refers back to the carriage ride and the horses, and makes a point that the horses were going in the direction of *eternity*.

- *Who is the speaker?* The speaker is a person recalling this event, which happened "centuries" before. Therefore the speaker has already died and is now existing in some kind of afterlife that is not described.

Step 3: Figurative Language

Death is *personified* here as the carriage driver. Students already will be aware of another and much scarier personification of death—namely, the Grim Reaper. The carriage ride is the speaker's journey from this life into the afterlife. That the horses are pointed toward eternity is a good clue that this is not an ordinary carriage ride and that the ride is more likely to be an image the poet is using to convey something *extra*ordinary.

Other important images: in addition to describing in detail the carriage driver and the ride itself, the class should take some time to focus on the significance of what the speaker is wearing (stanza four); the articles of clothing add up to a picture of a *bride*.

Step 4: Abstract

Through her use of personification, Emily Dickinson presents her readers with a depiction of death. Unlike many representations of death that are menacing or frightening, however, Emily Dickinson's Death is a kind, gentleman carriage driver—more seductive than terrifying.

We often see the metaphor of "life as a journey" in poetry; here the metaphor is extended to include the experience of death—and death as a journey in its own right. The speaker of the poem travels through life and then takes this final journey that offers her a whole new perspective on the life she already has experienced. Like a young bride, she begins a new life; in this case, she is beginning a new life in the unknown hereafter.

More On Age-Appropriate Metaphors

At this age level, a teacher should avoid elaborating too much on the visual Dickinson gives us of the rider as a bride. At higher grade levels, it is not unusual for a discussion of this poem to include something about the "Bride of Christ" image, as religious readings of Dickinson poems are not uncommon; for older high school students, a discussion of this nature could be fruitful.

However, what would be appropriate and useful to explore with a middle school class would be the image of the setting sun. A day's cycle as a metaphor for a lifespan is one they will undoubtedly see again—dawn, analogous to birth; and sunset, to one's death. Similar type "cycle" metaphors might include the cycle of a week (the seven days in the Genesis creation story), the cycle of a storm, or the four seasons.

THE BIGGER PICTURE

Because students are likely to be puzzled at first by this poem with its slightly esoteric vocabulary, there is likely to be a wide range of responses about what its various pieces could possibly mean, before there is even talk about how all the pieces might fit together. It is important that, no matter how time-constrained the class, each student has a chance to voice those differing views, even if it means having to extend the discussion into the next class period.

After all is said and done, students will recognize the value of others' contributions. Individual perspectives will make putting together a more complete picture easier for them; especially when facing something a little puzzling or difficult (like a Dickinson poem), students will learn by experiencing firsthand that a little help from friends can go a long way.

Also, once the class works through the basics of each stanza and discussion shifts to focus on the poem's themes, a teacher can facilitate a conversation on the topic of the universality of death. No matter what his background, or how much money or power a person possesses, death visits us all (*see* Hamlet's famous gravedigger soliloquy[1]).

However unique the individual circumstances of death are for each of us, death is an experience we all have in common, though the individual circumstances will differ. Thus, with this classroom discussion, a teacher can reinforce the notion that we are all, in some fundamental ways, connected to each other. And this is what we mean when we talk about the universal human condition.

MORE ON PERSONIFICATION

In Dickinson's poem, we see the experience of death embodied in the person of a carriage driver. But personification is not limited to the embodiment of an experience or abstract idea. In Elizabeth Bishop's "The Fish," the speaker imposes some human traits on a fish. A teacher can draw a distinction with this poem, though: while Bishop's fish is given some human qualities, such aspects of the fish are clearly coming from the perspective of the speaker; this approach is quite different from simply anthropomorphizing the fish (which would attribute to it human traits and emotions), in which case it would more closely resemble a fish like Dory in Disney's *Finding Nemo*.

The Fish
I caught a tremendous fish
and held him beside the boat
half out of the water, with my hook
fast in a corner of his mouth.
He didn't fight.
He hadn't fought at all.
He hung a grunting weight,
battered and venerable
and homely. Here and there
like brown skin hung in strips
like ancient wallpaper:
shapes like full-blown roses
stained and lost through age.
He was speckled with barnacles,
fine rosettes of lime,
and infested
with tiny white sea-lice,
and underneath two or three

rags of green weed hung down.
While his gills were breathing in
the terrible oxygen
—the frightening gills,
fresh and crisp with blood,
that can cut so badly—
I thought of the coarse white flesh
packed in like feathers,
the big bones and the little bones,
the dramatic reds and blacks
of his shiny entrails,
and the pink swim-bladder
like a big peony.
I looked into his eyes
which were far larger than mine
but shallower, and yellowed,
the irises backed and packed
with tarnished tinfoil
seen through the lenses
of old scratched isinglass.
They shifted a little, but not
to return my stare.
It was more like the tipping
of an object toward the light.
I admired his sullen face,
the mechanism of his jaw,
and then I saw
that from his lower lip
—if you could call it a lip—
grim, wet, and weaponlike,
hung five old pieces of fish-line,
or four and a wire leader
with the swivel still attached,
with all their five big hooks
grown firmly in his mouth.
A green line, frayed at the end
where he broke it, two heavier lines,
and a fine black thread
still crimped from strain and snap
when it broke and he got away.
Like medals with their ribbons
frayed and wavering,
the five-haired beard of wisdom
trailing from his aching jaw.
I stared and stared

and victory filled up the boat,
from the pool of the bilge
where oil had spread a rainbow
around the rusted engine
to the bailer rusted orange,
the sun-cracked thwarts,
the oar-locks on their strings,
the gunnels—until everything
was rainbow, rainbow, rainbow!
And I let the fish go.

FOUR STEPS: THE FISH

Step 1: Vocabulary

New Vocabulary—venerable, barnacles, rosettes, entrails, peony, isinglass, sullen, bilge, thwarts, oar-locks, gunnels

Step 2: Literal

The speaker has caught a fish she or he describes as "tremendous," which makes the fish sound immediately like an impressive catch. However, in line 5, the speaker tells us that the fish did not put up a fight against being caught. In fact, the description of the fish in lines 10–64 makes the fish sound old, tired, and sick.

Because the poem is comprised of such a lengthy description, a teacher should help students break it down into manageable parts, even if it is not already broken up into stanzas for them, as the Dickinson poem was. A teacher also can help students sort through the details by asking them, for instance, to pinpoint specific characteristics of the fish as they are provided in the poem. For example, "infested with . . . sea-lice." (In addition, it can be helpful to write these words and phrases on the board.)

As the poem comes to its conclusion, after looking at and pondering this fish for a considerable amount of time, the speaker lets the fish go.

Step 3: Figurative Language

The fish is given characteristics of a person—more specifically, a war veteran complete with ribbons "commemorating" past battles. The struggle—or lack of struggle, as it were—also seems to suggest something more abstract. The rainbow at the end of the poem also is something that, at this in stage in the process, seems like it might warrant further consideration and discussion.

More on Figurative Language

An important part of the figurative language Bishop employs in this poem is her use of several *similes* (for example, the swim-bladder / like a big peony). Have students identify the similes; not only will this develop their appreciation for creative figurative language, but it also will help them become more adept at recognizing similes and distinguishing them from metaphors.

Step 4: Abstract

The literal story happening in this narrative poem is simple enough to understand. The ultimate question is why, at the end, does the speaker let the fish go? Asking this question can launch a full discussion of the subtleties in the description that create the poem's meaning. And, as the following illustrates, a teacher can use a series of questions to prompt students to dig deeper and consider all the angles of what seems like such a simple story on the surface.

To start, the first vocabulary word in step 1 is *venerable*. Using this word to describe the fish, as opposed to just *old*, implies a sense of respect for the fish. The fish is *honorable*. And although the fish does not put up a fight, it it not out of cowardice or weakness; in fact, the speaker spends most of the poem noticing all the evidence of the fish's former struggles that he has faced and survived.

Does the speaker throw the fish back into the water out of respect? Or does the speaker, still, simply throw the fish back into the water because there was no struggle and, as a result, no sense of victory? Perhaps the speaker relates to the fish as a survivor and empathizes with the fish enough to let it live. Or, perhaps it is out of a sense of communion with nature that the speaker lets the fish return to his natural environment, so that the fish can finish the course of his life as intended by nature.

The final section of the poem is more cryptic. In the last ten lines of the poem, the speaker emerges from his deep concentration on the fish and turns his/her attention to the surroundings. What does it mean to have the boat with its rusted engine surrounded by oil, which causes rainbows in the slick of the water's surface? Does the rusted boat somehow mirror the scarred fish?

And, to the poem's conclusion: what is the possible significance of the rainbows? Here, a teacher might first give a very scientific explanation of what rainbows are and how they occur; students might have insights based on this explanation as to why it serves as a good metaphor here. A teacher might also explain the rainbow as a well-recognized allusion to the biblical story of Noah and the covenant, and how the rainbow signified promise and hope, and trust between God (nature?) and people. Finally, a teacher could offer the more secular association of rainbows with beauty, and the peace that follows a storm. Taking all of these into account, we must ask a final question: what is the victory that suddenly fills the boat in line 66?

THE BIGGER PICTURE

With this lesson, students will learn (without the teacher having to state it outright) the power of asking questions and being willing to listen to a variety of answers. Indeed, the best analytical thinker is the one who asks the right questions—and does not necessarily always have the answers. As the students struggle together, they are reinforcing a sense of community; the shared struggle as it unfolds in the classroom in this way precipitates a victory of the most precious kind.

After discussing the various challenges and potential gains of multiple perspectives, students at this point in the program typically are becoming increasingly aware of themselves as members of a diverse group; with that growing self-awareness, they also are becoming more attentive to how they communicate and interact within the context of the group. They are learning about diversity, not just in theory but also in practice, as something relevant to their own daily experiences.

As students learn through the poems themselves about the different perspectives and voices that are in the world, as they listen in the classroom to the ideas of their classmates that might offer an insight they hadn't thought of themselves; moreover, as they experience the joy in being able to contribute to a discussion that gradually sheds light on a poem that looked impossible to decipher at first glance, they will develop a greater appreciation for a rainbow spectrum of views. And as students participate in these exercises and discussions, they are sure to develop a sense of interdependence with their classmates, so that they will experience firsthand the benefits of an environment that makes the most of its diversity.

NOTE

1. William Shakespeare, *Hamlet*, act 5, scene 1.

Lesson 5

Standardized Testing

Teachers are responsible for some key aspects of their students' development, beyond the most obvious requirement of imparting to them fundamentals of their own area—be it English, history, mathematics, or some other academic subject. It also goes beyond the other kinds of competencies discussed in this book, such as developing better interpersonal skills. There is also the matter of recognizing that a student in any teacher's care is at a very specific point in an ongoing education—meaning that teachers also are responsible, to some extent, for preparing students for whatever comes next along the academic path.

One of the increasing concerns in the existing education system is performance on various standardized tests. There is no denying the importance of the impact standardized test scores can have on students' lives and future academic careers. Therefore, in addition to wanting to meet the expectations of administration and parents, teachers naturally want to prepare students as best they can for whatever challenges come their way—even the standardized ones.

At the same time, the reality of standardized testing can present a dilemma: while teachers need to acknowledge the significance of these tests, it is also important to maintain that the primary goals in a classroom should be about imparting specific knowledge and developing students' skills as analytical thinkers; ultimately, we want students to gain the ability to take that knowledge and shape it for themselves. To teach with the goal of mastering a specific test seems counter to these objectives.

The good news is that it is possible to do both. By using a poetry program such as this one, students' vocabulary will grow; and they also will gain ample practice at close textual reading, which will undoubtedly help them when they are looking at reading passages and comprehension questions on tests—or word problems included in a math or analytical section.

While the study of poetry is quite enough in itself, it actually can be a fun and fruitful exercise to include a handful of mock test questions from time to time throughout the course of the poetry program. Using poems that are already part of the class syllabus as the focal point, a teacher can create short sets of questions that resemble the types of questions most commonly found on standardized tests.

For example, a handout with the following questions can be used as a follow-up exercise to Elizabeth Bishop's "The Fish."

Select the most appropriate answer for each question from the choices provided. You may refer back to the poem.

1. This poem would best be described as a(n):
   a. sonnet
   b. sestina
   c. epic poem
   d. narrative poem
2. The speaker lets the fish go because:
   a. it is wrong to kill a living thing
   b. the speaker has already achieved the thrill of catching the fish
   c. the speaker respects the fish as a survivor
   d. the fish is diseased
3. In line 8, the word *venerable* means:
   a. diseased
   b. honorable
   c. injured
   d. tired
4. The tone of the poem might be described as:
   a. hostile to nature
   b. sad
   c. sensitive to nature
   d. angry

Toward the end of the poetry program, it is often rewarding for students to write their own multiple choice questions for a poem before it is discussed. This kind of assignment helps them identify for themselves key features and ideas of a poem. Furthermore, it can be beneficial to allow time for the students' questions to be pooled and distributed to fellow classmates, or to organize students into pairs or smaller groups for them to quiz each other (for fun!). Any group work provides the bonus of developing students' ability for teamwork and increasing their sense of community. Let students become more aware of the role they play in *each other's* learning process.

Finally, worksheets like this one also might be assigned *before* discussing the poem as a class. Whether they answer the questions on their own or with one of their partners from the Appointment Book sheet they created at the start of this program, a quick set of questions at the start of class gets everyone thinking and working right away. The classroom immediately is a buzzing hive of activity and creativity.

In addition to the benefit of providing familiar material—in this case, "The Fish"—in an altogether different light, exercises featuring mock test questions will demystify the test-taking experience and increase confidence for when the real tests arrive. When creating questions, a teacher also can zero in on common mistakes and offer some strategies. For example, in question 2, while it may be true that it is wrong to kill a living thing (choice a), that statement is not the focus of this poem. When asked to describe the tone of a poem, as in question 4, it is unlikely that a correct answer ever will reflect any kind of prejudice or hostility. Other techniques—such as defining a word by context and using the process of elimination—are also worth reviewing with students.

The construction of mock tests thus affords a teacher the opportunity to create test questions that combine the testing of real knowledge (What is a *sestina*?) and reinforcing students' skills of interpretation, while at the same time providing students with practice in general test-taking techniques.

THE BIGGER PICTURE

The practice with such mock-test questions does much more than teach students how to get a higher score: it teaches them to consider options. It teaches them the value of being able to see things from an angle slightly different from their own, and of recognizing possible alternative views quickly, as timed test taking requires. And, specifically in the context of standardized testing, students' ability to shift their perspective from their own to consider things from the viewpoint of another—namely, the test *maker*—often can increase their chances of determining a correct answer. Thus, the potential benefit of remaining open to others' views is something the student experiences here in a very tangible, quantifiable way.

Lesson 6

Two Poems, Side by Side

Once students have become comfortable with the four-step method and have tackled a variety of poems, it is a good time to introduce the idea of how poems, when taken together, can enhance each poem's meaning for us. Up to this point, we have been loosely threading together the assigned poems by focusing on recurring themes, and also with our *Bigger Picture* discussions regarding the value of diversity. This lesson of pairing two poems, however, is different from the usual compare/contrast exercises. Using two poems such as William Blake's "The Lamb" and "The Tyger" will encourage students to consider how two poems can *complement* each other.

The Lamb
Little Lamb, who made thee?
Dost thou know who made thee?
Gave thee life and bid thee feed,
By the stream and o'er the mead;
Gave thee clothing of delight,
softest clothing wooly bright;
Gave thee such a tender voice,
Making all the vales rejoice!
Little lamb who made thee?
Dost thou know who made thee?

Little Lamb I'll tell thee,
Little lamb I'll tell thee!
He is called by thy name,
For he calls himself a Lamb:
He is meek and he is mild,
He became a little child:

I a child and thou a lamb,
We are called by his name.
   Little Lamb God bless thee.
   Little Lamb God bless thee.

The Tyger

Tyger! Tyger! burning bright
In the forests of the night,
What immortal hand or eye
Could frame thy fearful symmetry?

In what distance deeps or skies
Burnt the fire of thine eyes?
On what wings dare he aspire?
What the hand, dare seize the fire?

And what shoulder, & what art,
Could twist the sinews of thy heart?
And when thy heart begins to beat,
What dread hand? & what dread feet?

What the hammer? what the chain?
In what furnace was thy brain?
What the anvil? what dread grasp
Dares its deadly terrors clasp?

When the stars threw down their spears,
And water'd heaven with their tears,
Did he smile his work to see?
Did he who made the Lamb make thee?

Tyger! Tyger! burning bright
In the forests of the night,
What immortal hand or eye
Dare frame thy fearful symmetry?

Of course, before comparing the two poems, students first must consider each poem separately, using the four-step method. Hopefully, by this point, working the steps is almost second nature to them.

FOUR STEPS: THE LAMB

Step 1: Vocabulary

New Vocabulary—mead (here, short for meadow)

Step 2: Literal

The speaker of the poem, a child ("I a child") is speaking to a lamb. In the first stanza, she or he is asking the lamb about its creator, who gave the lamb all of the characteristics the speaker describes. In the second stanza, the speaker answers his or her own question; the creator is someone people also call a *lamb* (Christ, "Lamb of God"), and this lamb became a child (Jesus), just as the speaker is also a child.

Step 3: Figurative Language

The focus of the figurative language/symbolism in this poem is the lamb itself. The speaker clearly makes the connection between the lamb and the Christian image of God.

Step 4: Abstract

By focusing on the lamb and the "Lamb of God" image, the speaker is focusing on the benevolent nature of God and the gentleness of his creations. Furthermore, as God is depicted here as a lamb and as a child, he appears to dwell as part of all living things.

THE BIGGER PICTURE

"The Lamb" is excellent for reinforcing a sense of unity among the students. Not only does it seem to promote gentleness and goodwill among all living things, but it also hints at the idea that God—or, the creative force in the universe, since God is never named outright—exists in each of us. Regardless of one's religious background, this sense of connectedness is universal. Christian, Buddhist, atheist—we are all part of one humankind.

FOUR STEPS: THE TYGER

Step 1: Vocabulary

New Vocabulary—symmetry, aspire, sinews

Step 2: Literal

The speaker of this poem is speaking to a tiger. The first and the final stanzas are nearly identical, asking the question of its creator. The description of the creator, as the speaker tries to imagine him or her is as someone to be feared.

The speaker asks if the creator of the lamb and of the tiger are one and the same.

Step 3: Figurative Language

The central figure of this poem is the tiger. The tiger, as creation, is connected to the creator; the tiger, therefore, evokes an image of a creator/God who is as powerful and fierce as the creation itself.

Step 4: Abstract

The speaker makes a connection between creator and creation. In this poem, the creator of such an animal as a tiger is viewed as equally wild, intimidating, and strong. The poem refers back to the image of the gentle lamb ("Did he who made the lamb make Thee?")—and how that creation seems to show a different side to the creator that is more benevolent.

THE BIGGER PICTURE

Both lamb and tiger are beautiful creatures but harness their beauty and power in radically different ways. By considering two creations that seem to exist on opposite ends of the spectrum, and thus two opposing characterizations of the creator, the speaker of "The Tyger" is contemplating the duality present in the world, and also within each of us.

PUTTING IT TOGETHER

To begin a discussion that takes both poems into account, a teacher can begin as she would any compare/contrast discussion. Create two columns on the blackboard, one for "Similarities" and one for "Differences." The following are some possibilities:

Similarities

1. Both discuss the creator as well as the creation.
2. The speakers address the creations directly.
3. Both poems describe the attributes of the creation.
4. Both draw inferences about the nature of the creator based on the nature of the creation that is the subject of the poem.
5. Religious symbolism.
6. Use of repetition.

Differences

1. The natures of the creations are different (lamb is docile; tiger is fierce).
2. The natures of the creations suggest different "sides" to the creator (benevolent versus something to be feared).
3. "The Lamb" is comprised mostly of questions; "The Tyger" includes numerous exclamations.
4. Tone.

The speaker's pivotal question in "The Tyger" ("Did he who made the lamb make thee?") will aim the class discussion at considering the dual nature of all things—God, animals, people. Nothing, in fact, is all good or all bad. Nothing is all gentle or all terrifying. And this is how these two poems *taken together* convey Blake's ultimate meaning. While we have just shown, by using the four-step method, that these poems work well independently of each other, we also see how, as a pair, they bring to light a much greater idea.

It is important and central to this lesson that students understand that the second poem ("The Tyger") was written by the same poet, with the first poem in mind. Yet, a meaningful pairing also can result from poems written by different authors, when the second poem is a deliberate response to the first poem. For example, Christopher Marlowe's "Passionate Shepherd" and Sir Walter Raleigh's "Nymph's Reply" are a deliberate pairing and popular for class discussions; but they are more appropriate for older students. For a middle school student group, William Wordsworth's "The World Is Too Much with Us" coupled with Denise Levertov's "O Taste and See" provides ample discussion fodder while remaining age appropriate.

THE BIGGER PICTURE OF THE PAIR

"The Lamb" and "The Tyger" considered together can teach us a greater respect for the complex nature of all living things—that the contrasts in the world actually work together to make this world more interesting, more alive. The gentleness of the lamb is that much more recognizable *because* the tiger exists as a point of comparison. Ultimately, this pair of poems increases an awareness in ourselves of our own dual nature, our capacity to be both gentle and strong, which will hopefully increase our awareness and respect for the coexistence of these elements in those around us.

More on Pairing Texts

Pairing texts can open the door for many kinds of assignments and projects, especially when a teacher allows students the time and resources to do additional research to take into account other historical or social aspects reflected in the works. Again, the challenge for a teacher will be to curate the poems so that there are some very obvious connections, but then, for more astute students, there might be some underlying commonalities or differences to discover.

For example, a teacher might create a set of poems, each featuring two congruent moments in history, such as poems that offer a voice from the American Civil War (a good one for this age group, "Little Giffen" by Francis Orray Ticknor) paired with a voice from another era, such as "I Explain a Few Things" by Pablo Neruda (Spanish Civil War), or the modern voice presented in "God Has Pity on Kindergarten Children" by the Israeli poet Yehuda Amichai.

Lesson 7

Other Poems

At this point in the program, the teacher has provided students with a solid foundation in methodology and introduced them to a number of literary devices and concepts that will be useful tools in their analyses. Furthermore, class discussions and any individual written assignments thus far should have bolstered each student's confidence level as much as his or her skill set. The following additional poems recommended for further practice work well with this program and age level.

The Ball Poem

What is the boy now, who has lost his ball,
What, what is he to do? I saw it go
Merrily bouncing, down the street, and then
Merrily over—there it is in the water!
No use to say "O there are other balls":
An ultimate shaking grief fixes the boy
As he stands rigid, trembling, staring down
All his young days into the harbour where
His ball went. I would not intrude on him,
A dime, another ball is worthless. Now
He senses first responsibility
In a world of possessions. People will take balls,
Balls will be lost always, little boy,
And no one buys a ball back. Money is external.
He is learning, well behind his desperate eyes,
The epistemology of loss, how to stand up.
And gradually light returns to the street,
A whistle blows, the ball is out of sight,
Soon part of me will explore the deep and dark

Floor of the harbor . . . I am everywhere,
I suffer and move, my mind and my heart move
With all that move me, under the water
Or whistling, I am not a little boy.

(John Berryman)

FOUR STEPS: THE BALL POEM

Step 1: Vocabulary

New Vocabulary—epistemology

Step 2: Literal

A boy has lost his ball, which has bounced into the water. There is no consolation for the loss. At the end of the poem, the boy imagines himself on the floor of the harbor, under the water. He is no longer a little boy.

Step 3: Figurative Language

The ball here represents something that inevitably will be lost (any possession or something more abstract, such as innocence/childhood).

Step 4: Abstract

It may surprise teachers how well the young students relate to this poem. Despite their youth, all of the students have already experienced loss of some kind. They also are at an age when they are beginning to sense the loss of their childhood; their innocence is giving way to a more sophisticated view of the world around them. They understand the irrevocability of this loss, and of the irreplaceable quality of certain things and feelings.

The last five lines of the poem are a little more puzzling to young readers; the lines bring into question the identity of the speaker. While students are usually inclined to think of the speaker as a young boy, the last lines tend to make them reconsider and envision an older person looking back at himself as a child. This change in thought invites a discussion focused on the role memory can play in our interpretation of events. How similar is the perspective of an adult as he reflects on events that happened when he was a child to the perspective he held at the time it was happening? The perspective of a person, in fact, can evolve as time goes on, even when it concerns the perspective of a particular moment or event. Students should consider how experiences, as we accumulate them, can impact our perspective.

Thus, it is not only a matter of how individuals differ from each other, but also how one individual's perspective can be different—sometimes, wildly different—at different points in time. Revisit Hayden's poem "Those Winter Sundays" in which the adult speaker looks back on their childhood years with a fresh perspective on their father.

THE BIGGER PICTURE

As a student considers the dynamic nature of perspectives, he is likely to become less defensive about his own perspective and less concerned with proving the "right-ness" of his point of view—as he comes to the realization that even his own viewpoint is subject to change. This increased awareness is not only good for the sake of community, but it also can be very liberating for the individual student: a student breaks free of his (to borrow an image from poet Blake) "mind-forged manacles"; he will no longer limit himself—he gives himself the freedom to explore, appreciate, and perhaps even adopt for himself a new perspective.

To an Athlete Dying Young
The time you won your town the race
We chaired you through the marketplace;
Man and boy stood cheering by,
And home we brought you shoulder-high.

Today, the road all runners come,
Shoulder-high we bring you home,
And set you at the threshold down,
Townsman of a stiller town.

Smart lad, to slip betimes away
From field where glory does not stay
And early though the laurel grows
It withers quicker than the rose.

Eyes the shady night has shut
Cannot see the record cut,
And silence sounds no worse than cheers
After earth has stopped the ears:

Now you will not swell the rout
Of lads that wore their honors out,
Runners whom renown outran
And the name died before the man.

So set, before its echoes fade,
The fleet foot on the sill of shade,
And hold to the low lintel up
The still-defended challenge cup.

And round that early-laureled head
Will flock to gaze the strengthless dead,
And find withered on its curls
The garland briefer than a girl's.

(A. E. Housman)

FOUR STEPS: TO AN ATHLETE DYING YOUNG

Step 1: Vocabulary

New Vocabulary—laurel, renown, lintel, garland

Step 2: Literal

The first and second stanzas each describe a different type of procession. If a teacher points this out to the class, students will look back at the stanzas and should be able to distinguish between the victory parade and the funeral procession. The rest of the poem talks about how, by dying at an early age, the young athlete will not have to grow up watching younger generations break the records he has set, and he will not have to endure the reality of people eventually ceasing to cheer his name; he will be spared the bittersweetness of looking back on one's glory days.

Step 3: Figurative Language

The poem relies heavily on the contrast between the images of the parade and the funeral procession. However, the withering garland at the end of the poem presents the readers with a common metaphor of connecting the brevity of a flower's bloom to one's youth, beauty, or glory.

- *Who is the speaker?* The speaker of the poem is a detached observer who speaks to the young athlete as if he were still alive.

Step 4: Abstract

The death of the young athlete raises the greater question as to which kind of death is more tragic—death in one so young, or the long life of a person who outlives his moment of glory or peak of success. The crux of this poem is that it takes what would normally be considered a tragedy and turns it into somewhat of a relief. While most people would agree that an untimely death of a young person—especially of a young person who has gained recognition early on—is a tragedy, the speaker argues that the young athlete is *lucky* because he will be spared the experience of growing older and of having to watch his own glory fade, just as beauty fades from the withering flowers.

THE BIGGER PICTURE

This poem reinforces the notion that there are a number of ways to view one event. Even something as undeniably tragic as the death of a young person can be interpreted in another way from what would be the most immediate response. Nothing—no matter how black-and-white it seems—is without the possibility of being viewed from an alternative perspective. Here, students will see the validity not only of different views, but also of views completely contrary to each other. Acknowledging the "positive" side of the death does not mean having to completely reject the "tragic"; rather, the class should arrive at the conclusion that multiple perspectives—even when in opposition to each other—are not mutually exclusive.

Other Recommended Poems

The following additional poems are rich in content as well as strong in their potential for discussions about diversity and its value:

- "The Art of Losing" by Elizabeth Bishop
- "Lightnin' Blues" by Rita Dove
- "London" by William Blake
- "Dulce Et Decorum Est" by Wilfred Owen
- "Anecdote of the Jar" by Wallace Stevens
- "Piano" by D. H. Lawrence
- "Boy at the Window" by Richard Wilbur
- "The Cool Web" by Robert Graves
- "The Negro Speaks of Many Rivers" by Langston Hughes
- "Harlem" by Langston Hughes
- "The Thought-Fox" by Ted Hughes
- "This Is a Photograph of Me" by Margaret Atwood
- "How to Write a Poem about the Sky" by Leslie Marmon Silko
- "beware   :   do not read this poem" by Ishmael Reed

These poems represent a variety of time periods, styles, and cultural backgrounds. Certainly, there are myriad poems that could be good choices, keeping in mind that the goal is to expose students to a wide range of voices—the more perspectives, the better. The poems suggested above vary in terms of their level of difficulty, which means in some cases a teacher may have to do more prompting than in others. A couple examples of this follow:

- Stevens's "Anecdote of the Jar," though simple and straightforward in its language, may be difficult in concept for students. It may take some extra prompting from a teacher for them to grasp that the displaced jar's relation to the natural environment is the crux of this poem. But once this hurdle is met, it can lead to an engaging *Bigger Picture* discussion about the interplay between person and environment, and the impact context can have on our own perspective of someone or something.
- Graves's "The Cool Web" is another example of a more difficult poem that is well worth the effort: by offering a little extra guidance, a teacher can facilitate a lively class discussion focused on the nature and role of language in society.

Naturally, a teacher wants to be in tune with the individual and collective capabilities of students, using discretion when deciding what poems to use and how much of a helping hand to offer. It is a delicate balance: we want the process to be challenging for students, but when the challenge tips too far toward frustration we run the risk—especially with younger students—of turning them off to poetry entirely. And even A. E. Housman could not convince us of a brighter side to such a tragic turn.

Lesson 8

One More Favorite

The following poem by Nora Dauenhauer is the perfect bookend to the Reading Poems portion of this program, with its focus on diversity. Naturally, it is important for a teacher to draw from multicultural texts in an attempt to expose students to different voices. And Dauenhauer's poem, as a Native American voice, is a good addition to the mix of poems already covered. Still building on what has already been explored, however, this poem offers something unique to the class: it presents cultural heritage (and identity) as something dynamic, something that persists in the face of great obstacles.

At the heart of this poem is the theme of tradition and rituals, how they allow us to protect and pass on, from one generation to the next, a sense of who we are and where we came from—something each student undoubtedly will relate to, whatever his or her personal background. It addresses the merits of respecting traditions while at the same time letting them evolve. Because, in fact, it is only if we let them evolve that they stand any chance of surviving the changing times.

As a way of wrapping up this part of the program, a teacher might more loosely apply the four-step method, well-practiced by now: Rather than having students write down the four steps as they have been doing, simply use the steps to steer a class discussion—starting with the vocabulary and use of Native American words, pointing out the literal "recipe" structure, and then moving into a full discussion of how the two recipes function as metaphors (figurative language) and possible interpretations.

How to Make Good Baked Salmon from the River
for Simon Ortiz
and for all our friends and relatives
who love it

67

It's best made in dry-fish camp on a beach by a
fish stream on sticks over an open fire, or during
fishing, or during cannery season.

In this case, we'll make it in the city baked in
an electric oven on a black fry pan.

INGREDIENTS
Barbecue sticks of alder wood.
In this case, the oven will do.
Salmon: River salmon, current supermarket cost
$4.99 a pound.
In this case, salmon poached from river.
Seal oil or olachen oil.
In this case, butter or Wesson oil, if available.

DIRECTIONS
To butcher, split head up the jaw. Cut through,
remove gills. Split from throat down the belly.
Gut, make sure you toss all to the seagulls and
the ravens because they're your kin, and make sure
you speak to them while you're feeding them.
Then split down along the back bone and through
the skin. Enjoy how nice it looks when it's split.

Push stake through flesh and skin like pushing
a needle through cloth, so that it hangs on stakes
while cooking over fire made from alder wood.

Then sit around and watch the slime on the salmon
begin to dry out. Notice how red the flesh is,
and how silvery the skin looks. Watch and listen
to the grease crackle, and smell its delicious
aroma drifting around on a breeze.

Mash some fresh berries to go along for dessert.
Pour seal oil in with a little water. Set aside.

In this case, put the poached salmon in a fry pan.
Smell how good it smells while it's cooking,
because it's soooooooo important.

Cut up an onion. Put in a small dish. Notice how
nice this smells too and how good it will taste.

Cook a pot of rice to go along with salmon. Find
some soy sauce to put on rice, maybe borrow some.

In this case, think about how nice the berries would
have been after the salmon, but open a can of fruit
cocktail instead.

Then go out by the cool stream and get some skunk
cabbage, because it's biodegradable, to serve the
salmon from. Before you take back the skunk cabbage
you can make a cup out of one to drink from the
cool stream.
In this case, plastic forks, paper plates and forks will do, and
drink cool water from the faucet.

TO SERVE
After smelling smoke and fish and watching the
cooking, smelling the skunk cabbage and the berries
mixed with seal oil, when the salmon is done, put
the salmon on stakes on the skunk cabbage and pour
some seal oil over it and watch the oil run into
the nice cooked flaky flesh which has now turned
pink.

Shoo mosquitoes off the salmon, and shoo the ravens
away, but don't insult them because the mosquitoes
are known to be ashes of the cannibal giant,
and Raven is known to take off with just about
anything.

In this case, dish out on paper plates from fry pan.
Serve to all relatives and friends you have invited
to the barbecue and those who love it.

And think how good it is that we have good spirits
that still bring salmon and oil.

TO EAT
Everyone knows that you can eat just about every
part of the salmon, so I don't have to tell you
that you start with the head because it's everyone's
favorite. You take it apart bone by bone, but make
sure you don't miss the eyes, the cheeks, the nose
and the very best part—the jawbone.

You start on the mandible with a glottalized
alveolar fricative action as expressed in the Tlingit
verb als'oos'.

Chew on the tasty, crispy skins before you start
on the bones. Eeeeeeeeeeeee!!!! How delicious.

Then you start on the body by sucking on the fins
with the same action. Include crispy skins, then
the meat with grease dripping all over it.

Have some cool water from the stream with the salmon.

In this case, water from the faucet will do.
Enjoy how the water tastes sweeter with the salmon.

When done, toss the bones to the ravens and
seagulls and mosquitoes, but don't throw them in
the salmon stream because the salmon have spirits
and don't like to see the remains of their kin
among them in the stream.

In this case, put bones in plastic bag to put
in dumpster.

Now settle back to a story telling session, while
someone feeds the fire.

In this case, small talk and jokes with friends
will do while you drink beer. If you shouldn't
drink beer, tea or coffee will do nicely.

Gunalchéesh for coming to my barbecue.

DISCUSSION POINTS

Another fish poem. Another LONG fish poem. Actually, if at least one student makes this remark, a teacher should smile because it indicates the student is making connections between the poems the class has studied and the metaphors and imagery contained within them. Moreover, it opens the door for a teacher to point out how images can have different meanings and purposes in poems. The fish in Elizabeth Bishop's poem, and the *themes* of that poem, are very different from those here.

An important reason why "How to Make Good Baked Salmon" gets status as a favorite for this program is because it seems to go against all the earlier misconceptions about what makes a poem a poem. Remember William Carlos Williams's "This Is Just to Say" from earlier? Well, here we have another poem where the language is as plain as an everyday note; it appears at first glance to be little more than an annotated recipe. And a very long set of instructions at that.

On the literal level, this poem does, in fact, alternate between two recipes: one is the traditional recipe that is reminiscent of a time when Native Americans lived in harmony with nature; the second recipe is a modern version, altered to accommodate limited resources of city life and to make use of modern conveniences and store-bought items.

The second (modern day) recipe is easier, described as "good enough"— implying something has been compromised. So there's a question for the class: what has been lost? However, the new recipe makes the tradition more suited to the here and now, so more likely to survive for generations to come. Were the speaker, or others, married to the specifics of the ritual of old, the tradition would have to be thrown away once a person no longer lived near a river where salmon could be caught; more important, the higher purpose of the ritual—the sense of connectivity it expresses and reinforces—would be lost.

With the specificity of the recipe instructions, it is clear that the preparation process is as important as the resulting dish. Within the preparation are moments that reinforce ideas about kinship with other living things, respect for the animals and the natural world. Also an integral part of the preparation is its emphasis on taking time to fully appreciate the details, such as how the water tastes sweeter with the salmon. The time involved in this ritual, in fact, is a key aspect of the power of tradition: beyond ensuring someone takes their time during the preparation stage, the instructions emphasize the communal nature of the meal. Once your salmon is done, be sure to take the time to share it. Thus, the importance of gathering together family and friends for food and conversation; strengthening our sense of community and our connection with loved ones; sharing perspectives around a table. And so, the individual and collective stories live on.

Students do not need to be Native American to understand the importance of traditions as a way of honoring one's roots and that part of their own identity. Discussion can focus on the traditions and little rituals each of their own families maintains—whether it's about how they celebrate holidays or how they build a sand castle together each summer on the first day at the beach. From there, the discussion can broaden from families to communities. Consider local football or hockey games that bring people together: picture multiple generations all sporting the home team's colors, shouting and clapping the hometown cheer, and perhaps even dancing along with the team mascot.

THE BIGGER PICTURE

While day-to-day circumstances and rituals of people may be vastly different from each other (even within in a single cultural group, as exemplifid in this poem), we all share a similar purpose: to feel connected, to experience ourselves as part of something bigger and lasting. Poetry not only expresses this aspect of humanity but, by opening up our individual world to a kaleidescope of other perspectives, it also enables us to achieve this end.

Building Confidence

Homework and Feedback

Plenty of debate is out there regarding homework—how much is too much, how much is too little, the right combination of short-term assignments and long-term projects, and so forth. Especially at the middle school level, the homework load is expected to increase as greater emphasis is placed on developing a student's organization and time-management skills. Despite this pressure on teachers to assign something "substantial" each night as part of the student's workload, however, the truth is that assigning any more than a couple of poems (depending on their length and level of difficulty) will not be productive.

At first, students will be elated to see they only have to read two poems for homework. However, they will almost instantly learn that those two poems are going to require quite a bit more of their time than they may have realized: for, what will become the core of any assignment will be the documentation of their working through the four steps and keeping their work organized in a notebook that can be submitted periodically so a teacher can easily monitor effort (note: not grading for content here). Writing out a four-step response to each poem as part of the homework translates into students arriving to class with a prep sheet in hand for group discussion: it gives them a chance to sort through and solidify ideas beforehand, consider aspects of the poem they think are particularly noteworthy, and get a little more curious about what others in the class will have to say.

Students should be encouraged as much as possible during this stage of the learning process, so that working through the four steps and developing an interpretation of a poem does not turn into too daunting an experience. Teachers should offer ample verbal praise and prompt students before they become frustrated. *All* students are capable of some level of analysis, but a teacher will need to be sensitive to the range of capabilities in a class and ensure that each student feels validated in his or her response to the the material.

Thinking abstractly seems like shaky ground to students who have been, up until this stage in their academic careers, working mostly with the literal details of texts, usually in the form of comprehension questions or book reports. And as some students begin to turn the proverbial corner, a teacher will need to further encourage the others by assuring them patience and perseverance are the only magic they will need to get them there, too. However, beyond responding to a teacher's prompting and encouragement, students also need to learn how to push themselves beyond the obvious, to go to that edge. To not settle for the first interpretation that comes to them with just a glance at a poem.

In doing these homework assignments, students should steadily gain confidence in their abilities to interpret a poem by using the four-step method. Their confidence will be reinforced twofold when they hear their own ideas—as they are written down in their homework notebooks—articulated by fellow classmates. Gradually, they will lose the sense that they are out on a limb alone. Periodic checking of notebooks will allow a teacher to assess individual progress and troubleshoot any stumbling blocks before they get too big. Students should understand that, as abstract thinking is something new to them, they can expect to have some difficulty (and missteps!) in making the leap from the literal, especially in the beginning.

Ultimately, assignments and subsequent discussions work toward getting students to a point where they feel secure about their own instincts and ideas. With this level of confidence, they are less likely to feel a need to negate the perspectives of others; and they are more likely to be enthusiastic about entertaining the ideas of others, particularly when a classmate comes up with an idea they hadn't thought of themselves.

In addition to requiring students to document their four-step work in a notebook as homework, a teacher might occasionally assign a short homework assignment in the form of a personal reflection. An important aspect of poetry is its power to evoke emotions; and some quiet time to themselves, outside of the classroom, could be the perfect opportunity for students to explore that more comfortably. Also, a personal response assignment will help students learn the distinction between a formal interpretation of a literary work, which adheres closely to the text, and an equally valid but altogether different kind of response focused more on the reader's personal reaction. (Note, however, that a reflection piece is still a formal piece of writing—a far cry from the informal, in-class journal writing discussed in the following chapter.)

As noted, it is recommended for teachers to collect notebooks periodically; but checking notebooks should only be to ensure students are, in fact, making a genuine effort to work through the four steps for each poem assigned. While feedback is vital to anyone's progress, grading homework assignments in this context will not be particularly helpful for most students and may even be counterproductive. If students know they will be graded on the content, students may become too focused on trying to figure out the "right" response for the best grade. In doing so, they may limit themselves in terms of their ideas; and limited ideas, in turn, will mean much more reserved—far less rewarding—class discussions.

In other words, while a teacher in class should prompt students with questions to encourage them to "dig deeper" or to keep their interpretation cohesive, students need to think of homework assignments as a time for brainstorming or exploration. Give them the space to try, to stretch. Otherwise, they will hold themselves back for fear of criticism or potentially jeopardizing their overall grade in the class.

Most of the time, simply noting whether or not the assignment has been completed with satisfactory effort will be enough; later in the program, a grading system of check−/check/check+ can be effective as incentive, as it will differentiate between those who are making great strides and those who are simply plodding along. In the end, the degree of effort that students have put into their homework assignments likely will be reflected in their performance on class tests and in whatever writing they submit for an actual grade.

Writing Assignments and Poet Project

Besides needing continuing practice in using the four-step method, students also need consistent practice in articulating their ideas through the use of proper sentence structure and paragraph formation. For this reason, several short writing assignments on a weekly basis are helpful. Regular writing assignments will allow students to take all the information they have collected and thread those pieces together into a cohesive idea or argument. And, as already discussed in the context of homework notebooks, written assignments keep students accountable, making sure they are not taking advantage of having short reading assignments by rushing through the expected work in a matter of minutes.

In the beginning, the assignments can be as simple as stating the central metaphor of a poem and discussing what it suggests on an abstract level. These short assignments also can be shared with the rest of the class and used to generate discussions. Later in the program, after the students have several poems in their knowledge bank, they can compare and contrast, or talk about a couple of poems based on a common theme.

When they do start writing about more than one poem in their writing assignments, it is important for a teacher to review paragraph formation and organization—a strong, clear thesis sentence for each paragraph's main idea followed by supporting sentences. A paragraph is best thought of as a mini-essay in itself: one idea presented, followed by details to support that idea, and finished off with a clear, concise conclusion that goes a little bit beyond just restating the opening sentence. No more, no less.

Most importantly, a teacher must insist on *direct* as well as indirect evidence from the text to support a student's main points. Like a good court case, the case to be made about a poem must be substantiated. Even if what the student asserts is perfectly obvious, it must be supported with evidence from the text. A teacher is interested in what the student can *prove*. Thus, the student must pay close attention to the text—this is what it means to be a critical reader. To this extent, such a detailed approach could result in focusing on a single word or phrase for an entire paragraph, or become the axis for an entire essay.

All this goes toward developing a cohesive interpretation of the poem. Once a student has asserted an idea and cited direct and indirect evidence from the text, his or her goal is to offer an explanation of *how* the textual evidence cited connects to the assertion. Students must learn to anticipate their readers' questions, since they are not likely to be around to explain their reasoning when their interpretation is being read. This is another way in which working with poetry, including these kinds of written assignments, increases awareness among students about the existence of multiple perspectives and the range of responses possible to any given one.

A LESSON ON CITATION

In addition to insisting on direct evidence in order to keep students disciplined in their approach, a teacher should use these assignments as a vehicle for teaching students early on about proper citation. Especially in an age where so much information is just a few clicks or a download away, practice in citation is essential because it develops a necessary respect for intellectual property. Giving credit where credit is due should become second nature to them; and it is a commendable quality that should carry over into their everyday lives.

For teachers who are breaking citation ground at the same time the class is just beginning to explore poetry, begin by having students cite under step 2 (literal) for a few assignments before upping the ante to require citation under step 4. In other words, have them document lines in the poem where the *literal* details they make note of are located. As they grow more comfortable with the process and format, students likely will realize that citation is well worth the effort because they will recognize how providing "evidence" adds to the credibility of their assertions.

IN-CLASS JOURNALS

In-class writing in the form of an ongoing journal is encouraged in this program. More specifically, short intervals (usually about five minutes) of constant free-writing. While these should be periodically collected and checked to ensure that the writing is happening, these are less about generating quality content than they are about getting students to just keep writing.

Keep the pen to the paper and keep it moving—students will be challenged to press on when they might otherwise get stuck because they are trying to think things all the way through, or come up with the exact way they want to express something, before committing to an idea in writing. As they learn more about the writing process they will learn there will be time later to organize, refine, revise (and scrap!) a lot of what they have written down. As the saying goes, there are no good writers—only good rewriters.

The benefits of casual, quick journaling are maximized when this exercise is done almost daily. A five-minute block of time at the start of a class period is a great way to get the class immediately on task, with a simple prompt to write something about the previous night's assignment; or, it can be used at any time within the class period preceding a class discussion, as a way of getting each student to jot down at least a few ideas they can then contribute.

As a quick prep for class discussion, the journal exercise can be very effective, especially with more reticent students: even if a teacher calls on a student directly rather than waiting for a raised hand, the student then has his journal to look back to for some ideas to share, and so he will not feel so put on the spot.

By keeping journal writing limited to these brief in-class times, a teacher also is more likely to avoid a dilemma that can develop when students journal outside of class—where they are more likely to treat the journal like a diary. First, we want to be consistent in the lesson that good critical reading and writing remains anchored in a text; even the more personal "reflection" writing assignments, as discussed, are required to stay focused on the assigned poem. However, just as important for practical reasons, teachers also want to avoid situations where writing might become so personal that information revealed is awkward, inappropriate, or alarming.

POET PROJECT

Toward the end of the Reading Poems portion of this program, a very productive assignment can take the shape of a Poet Project that allows students to work in pairs or small groups and focus their attention on one poet whose selected work already has been discussed in class. The assignment is as follows:

• Using books, magazines, and websites, research the poet's life, which may include a brief history of the time period.

- Produce fully developed interpretations of two poems by the poet (other than the poem or poems previously discussed in class).
- Create a poster using pictures, text, or other materials that feature the poet, poems, or highlights of aspects of your interpretations.
- Give a presentation to the class, using all your prepared materials. Your presentation should include leading a brief discussion (about ten minutes) on one of the two poems you have chosen to include in your project.

Discussions born out of this project can get quite spirited, as students are just learning how to facilitate a large group—hence the reason for keeping them relatively brief, but long enough to sufficiently wrap things up. Teachers should anticipate that students will refer back to the poem(s) by that poet already discussed as a class . . . and that is a good thing.

The ultimate goal of this project assignment is that, at the close of each presentation, students will have gotten a glimpse of a couple of other works of a poet, may have a slightly better sense of the poet and his or her body of work, and might be intrigued enough to do some additional reading on their own.

Technology, Multimedia,
and Teamwork

The ubiquitous use of technology—from smart phones to iPads—by students even at this young age has brought with it two things that teachers may not have had when they were the same age: speed of communication, which can be as instant and fleeting as a "snapchat"; and an audience that can reach literally into the millions. Moreover, our students are no longer limiting themselves to a select universe of "friends" (however broadly we now define that term), but also opening up themselves to conversations that include total strangers, even if it is just to play a game like Minecraft or share a video on YouTube of a school science project.

This is the reality that our students live in today. So where does poetry have a place in the midst of all this? More important, perhaps, is this question: How can the omnipresence of technology enhance our experience of poetry inasmuch as poetry enhances our ability to comprehend and savor the world around us? Poetry—reading it, writing it—gets students to slow down. It gets them to slow down their thought process, by compelling them to look more closely at what they are saying and trying to say. Poetry discussions can bring back an intimacy to conversations where students will be able to let go of the image or online persona they have created for themselves. It's a different kind of self-consciousness, and a vulnerability not experienced when communicating online or via social media.

At the same time, the aspect of our culture that has become quasi-confessional may make it easier for students to access that part of poetry that focuses on emotions. Poetry, in this way, becomes effective in helping students develop the ability not only to sort through various, sometimes competing, emotions and thoughts; it also can help them distinguish between responses based on emotions and more rationally based responses, which is a good skill to have in any form of communication.

USE OF TECHNOLOGY IN ASSIGNMENTS

The exciting thing about teaching today's tech-savvy young students is that, when it comes time for projects and presentations, teachers and students have all kinds of resources to explore together. With such a cornucopia of resources at their fingertips, students are given the opportunity to make poetry not only a creative experience in its own right, but also a more personal experience. Some ideas about how to incorporate technology use in your lesson plans include the following:

1. *Researching Subject Matter:* researching a certain topic or subject matter that either is a focus of a poem discussed in class or of a poem that the student would like to write.

   Subsequently, one might discuss how additional information factored into an interpretation of the poem and, if at all, changed the student's perspective. If the student is researching a topic before writing their own poem, it will enable them to have a more detailed understanding of their subject matter and perhaps lead to more descriptive language or creative images in their own expression.

2. *Pictures:* offering students various pictures of a poem's subject, person, or place mentioned can make it more "real" for a student. A teacher might experiment with differences in presenting pictures before reading a poem versus afterward.

   Also, there can be a discussion about the strengths of one medium in comparison to others; or how use of two forms considered together offers a perspective that is greater than the sum of its parts. Good examples of such coupling include showing students photographs of Mont Blanc after reading Shelley's poem of the same title; various depictions of the Virgin Mary cradling her dead son, including Michelangelo's sculpture, alongside Jorie Graham's poem "Pieta"; photographs of the Parthenon sculptures and the Parthenon itself, presented with Keats's "On Seeing the Elgin Marbles." You get the idea.

3. *Artifacts:* Have students write a poem about a photograph, painting, or piece of sculpture after an excursion to a nearby museum or gallery. Let the students sit with an object and write on their own. In this way, they may experience an almost meditative quality to their writing. If this activity follows an online activity of coupling pictures and words, a teacher can facilitate a discussion about how the two types of interaction with artwork—online and in person—differ, touching on the benefits and drawbacks of each. In this comparison discussion, address the issue of accessibility to art; now that so much is available online, consider how art enriches our lives and is, arguably, *necessary* for everyone . . . and why.

MULTIMEDIA PROJECTS

One way to encourage students to explore technology and multimedia expression is with a collage project. Have students create collages based on a poem and their interpretation of that poem; the collages can be comprised of words, pictures, textiles, artifacts, or any other materials they think express something about the poem. They can then present their collage to the class after they have read the poem and offered a brief interpretation.

Collage as an art form may be new to many or all of the students, so this is an assignment best approached in a few steps, such as these:

1. *Pictures:* using magazines, newspapers, or the Internet, cut out images that in some way relate to your poem; this can include the image of something (person, place, or thing) directly mentioned in your poem, or express something about the poem in a more abstract way, such as a picture of something you feel conveys the poem's tone.
2. *Words:* using magazines, newspapers, or the Internet, cut out words that in some way relate to your poem; rather than finding the same words that already appear in the poem, find ones that are *your own* but that you personally connect with the poem. In your presentation, you can explain why you associate the words you've chosen with the poem.
3. *Textiles and Artifacts:* Using things with texture—fabric, wood, cotton, grains, everyday objects, and so forth—you can add to your collage in a meaningful way that will bring your personal interpretation of the poem to life! Perhaps there is something in the poem or about the poem that makes you want to include pieces of an artifact in your collage. Don't be afraid to be extra creative. Have fun with it!

Note: not everyone will use textiles and artifacts, but all should include both images and words. In terms of grading, while a teacher may be quick to praise those who use extra materials, she or he should not require those extras for a good grade.

MULTIMEDIA: A RECOMMENDATION

A collection of poems recommended to illustrate the fun of creating multimedia projects is a slim volume titled *Mud Woman*, which is a collection of poems by the Native American poet Nora Naranjo-Morse. The poems appear alongside colorful, playful sculptures she has done that capture aspects of the culture and community she is trying to express.

TECHNOLOGY IN COLLABORATIVE PROJECTS

In addition to multimedia projects, which may be done by individuals or in groups, it can be very rewarding for students to work together on projects in which they connect a poem or set of poems with a specific social, cultural, or ethnic context. Or, students together could use poetry as a way of exploring a social justice topic in greater depth.

Using technology and delving into different forms of expression on a topic (which, thanks to the Internet, can be accessible to students in both urban and rural classrooms), can be an enriching team activity. Notably, this includes the ability to experience the perspectives of cultures that until recently relied so heavily on oral tradition that gaining such insight was nearly impossible. Technology, when used thoughtfully, becomes a window to the world; a teacher can guide students to ensure its proper use and, in this way, maximize the impact that worldview will have on her or his students' own perspective.

Collaborative projects that incorporate multimedia components allow students to take on different roles and explore forms of expression that might be quite foreign to them. Any assessment should take into account the attempts to be creative, even if the results are not always the prettiest to look at in the end. It might be wise for a teacher to think of an activity such as this one, rather than as an assignment, as the newest "great experiment."

COLLABORATIVE PROJECT IDEA: HISTORICAL FIGURES PANEL

Another activity centered around a social issue incorporates an exploration of historical figures while having some fun with role-playing. Have students assume various roles—for example, if focused on the topic of slavery or racism, a student can take on the role of Abraham Lincoln, Frederick Douglass, Martin Luther King Jr., or Harriet Tubman. Students should research thoroughly in order to have a well-rounded historical context for their characters, including significant events surrounding the figure's personal life details.

This kind of activity is extremely worthwhile as it gets students to adopt a perspective other than their own; and some of them—in order to create a more dynamic presentation—can take on the voice of a speaker that might be at odds with their own personal view (e.g., a slaveholder). Also, figures can come together who didn't even exist at the same time (e.g., Lincoln and Malcolm X) to discuss a set of poems. Begin with each one giving his or her own take on the poems, and then let the characters engage in a discussion where they are reacting and responding to each other.

An important part of this kind of project will be a subsequent discussion where the students get to discuss their experiences taking on those different roles, with time for them to commend their classmates regarding specific ways each captured his character's perspective and voice.

An alternative idea does not involve role-playing, and so may be better suited to certain groups or settings: a teacher can present a set of poems that all deal with a particular event in history, whether it's the Civil War or something more recent, and let students explore that one instance from various viewpoints.

ONLINE COLLABORATION

Especially because so much of modern communication and teamwork in the adult world happens virtually, the need for students to refine their online communication skills cannot be overstated. Whether it is a matter of quick text exchanges or e-mails, brief notes sent back and forth as incremental tasks of a larger project are getting delegated and accomplished, or more thought-out, drafted messages as elaborate designs are being laid out and negotiated, an individual must be able to navigate these waters.

In this spirit, a teacher might assign a small segment of a larger assignment to be carried out online—and ask that a transcript of the online communication be submitted along with other materials, as part of the overall assessed work. This is a terrific way to document the creative process and, upon review after the fact, it may help a student recognize strengths and weaknesses not only in terms of the process as a whole, but also more specifically of his or her part in it.

A caveat to teachers to not over-rely on virtual activity—students most likely will be more than happy to do the bulk of their work in this modern-day comfort zone! Rather, by touching on it lightly, teachers will help students recognize the real-life application of this kind of work while at the same time making them aware of the perks and pitfalls of virtual communications. Indeed, a text or e-mail is quick and easy to write, and it almost certainly will yield the most immediate response; but these quick exchanges also are most susceptible to misunderstandings and miscommunications.

THE BIGGER PICTURE:
MORE ON TEAMWORK AND ROLES

Collaborative projects and presentations, such as those suggested here, provide a unique opportunity to enable students to hone their skills in team building, indisputably a key component of any skill set that teachers can help students build for themselves. We live in a world of teams—not just team building for a particular school or work project; rather, our world today is one that makes it essential for people to know how to work in cross-functional teams. So it is crucial that students develop the understanding that each person has something to bring to the table for any given project—and often it is just a matter of figuring out what that is—and allowing space within the team framework for him or her to contribute.

Teams are always changing, so students need every opportunity possible to learn how to adapt more quickly and how to get along with others, often rising above personality quirks or different work styles. Being quick to recognize individual strengths is an invaluable trait—or a learned skill, if it does not come to a student innately. By utilizing the best of what each person has to offer, a team will benefit in terms of its work flow as well as its end product.

Understanding that a team is composed of many roles, in terms of process as well as deliverables, is an important lesson: some members will be better at things like organizing and documenting, while others will be quicker at hands-on tasks or specifics such as creating visuals or graphic designs. It is therefore beneficial for students to learn what roles on a team work best for them, which ones do not, and also to recognize those qualities in their peers. The teacher's role in this context is to encourage students, from project to project, to try different roles, with the understanding that some team positions, for each student, will be a better fit than others.

As students take on these various roles, a teacher should let team members work out the kinks on their own. It is a good life lesson for students to experience being a bit out of their comfort zone, and then trying to negotiate a bit if they can. Drastic changes in roles should be a last resort, reserved for when a student is feeling so overwhelmed or out of his or her element that the negative feeling will overshadow any positives to be gained. Students can negotiate these changes themselves but often will require some guidance from a neutral third-party—namely, the teacher.

Getting students to try on different "hats" in collaborative projects, especially complex projects that incorporate the use of technology, will help them develop a greater appreciation for all that goes into one thing—a poem, a project, or anything else; in this way, they also will come to a greater appreciation for the contribution any one person can make as part of a team. Should this exercise reveal a unique talent or strength that up until now remained undiscovered or untapped, all the more reason to celebrate the creative process and the wellspring of diversity all around us.

More on Student Assessments

A key to any teacher's success in this kind of a program is creating an atmosphere that provides structure and direction for the students while also offering up the time as an active experiment, a forum of ideas. A student needs to know that he can express an idea without risk of ridicule or criticism from the teacher or his peers. This does not give students free reign to express just any idea, however. A teacher should consistently follow up responses in class with the simple question, "Where do you see this in the text?" In doing so, a student will either be able to point to an image or metaphor and extrapolate or not.

In addition to participation in class, naturally there will be other criteria for assessing a student's performance throughout the program and on any oral or written work. A suggested rubric will include the following core components:

- *Content:* original and abstract ideas.
- *Organization and Development:* clear thesis statement; support ideas; direct evidence from the text.
- *Language, Mechanics, and Style:* sentence structure, punctuation, capitalization, and spelling; written in an appropriate formal style suited for literary analysis.
- *Quality of Research* (when part of assignment).
- *Use of Supplemental Materials* (optional).

Consider: how aware are students of any grading rubric a teacher is using to assess their performance and how familiar are they with its finer points? It is absolutely essential for a teacher to inform students ahead of time very specifically in what areas they will be assessed and how each of those areas will be weighted. And, especially with this age group, it will be important for a teacher, at regular intervals and for as long as the program lasts, to remind students of these specifics.

Just as important, directly in terms of the rubric, a teacher should provide incremental feedback for each student and to the group in terms of how they are working as a whole. This kind of feedback loop is at the heart of what we want perceived as an environment of fairness; and it also will alleviate any insecurities as students tackle uncharted territories—or, at least, areas that are not quite as objective and therefore not as easy for them to know where they stand.

Part II

WRITING POEMS

Once students have spent ample time reading and reflecting on poems written by others, they are ready to make a serious attempt at creating poems of their own. The time students spend reading poems necessarily comes first: it provides them with a range of poetry to use as models; it allows them to create a bank of images and metaphors; it develops a basic sense of language and rhythm; and it teaches them how to think abstractly. Above all, the time spent focused on reading poetry fosters an environment that respects any creative attempt, which in turn will allow students to feel comfortable enough to let themselves be vulnerable in their own writing, without having to worry about the reactions of their peers.

A teacher's approach in a conventional classroom setting with a typical school week schedule can be this straightforward: each Thursday, present the class with a handout that defines the type of poem for the week. Giving them the weekend to work on the poem(s) at their own pace, a teacher can set the due date for the following Monday. Depending on the length of the poem and the level of difficulty, it is generally a good rule of thumb to ask students to create two or three of each week's poetic form: assigning a few poems, rather than one, will give students more to choose from when the time comes for them to select poems to include in their final project.

Assigning the poems on the Thursday of each week gives students plenty of time (and the luxury of the weekend) to think of a subject and carefully craft each poem; even better than assigning on Friday, the extra weeknight gives them a better chance of going into the weekend already having given their poem some thought. And why not assign at the start of the week, to be handed in on Friday? Without having the space of the weekend to work the poems out, the writing assignment likely will become just one more thing to "get done" on a weekday night, squeezed in between other homework assignments, karate classes, or team sports. It is always the hope that the extra time and flexibility of the weekend schedule increases the likelihood students will experience a more intrinsically rewarding creative moment.

As for Mondays and what to expect during this poetry-writing extravaganza . . . well, a teacher should not be surprised to find that, in the upcoming weeks, the first day of the new week becomes one the students look forward to, as they often are eager to share their poems and hear what classmates have to offer. It can even get a little competitive, in a good way, with students trying to outdo each other with the more clever stanza or metaphor.

By assigning specific types of poems, a teacher is providing students with a structure—necessary as much for giving them some sense of security as it is to ensure they develop some technical skill. However, it is best to give students the freedom to write about things that actually matter to them. Going through the writing process from start to finish, which includes choosing their own subject matters, students can more fully experience the thrill of self-expression, as well as the hard work involved in producing something meaningful related to something they care about. This shared experience among the young poets inevitably creates a sense of solidarity among classmates as well as an appreciation for each other's efforts. While it is true that there often emerges some form of healthy competition among at least a few of the group, mostly a teacher will witness a sense of camaraderie in this endeavor.

On a final note regarding weekly assignments, in addition to providing students with a clear and concise definition of the week's poetic form, a teacher should provide the class with a few models. If available, it is helpful to show students work by previous students, as well as poems by well-known poets. Student examples can make the particular poetic form seem more accessible to the class, as something doable for someone their age and in their circumstances. Current students also will benefit in the post-writing class discussions when they hear their own classmates' creations. Classroom revelations often translate into inspiration for future assignments, and there is no better moment for a teacher than when she or he manages to set the stage for a student to be surprised by their own capabilites.

It is deliberate by design that the second part of this program relies on experiential learning. Students express their own ideas; in doing so, quite likely, they also reveal some underlying emotions in the process. And, as they struggle with using different poetic forms and witness their classmates going through the same thing, they are likely to develop a greater sense of empathy for those around them. Finally, as classmates listen to each other's poems and respond to them, students will experience a sense of validation from their peer group.

Essential to achieving the program's *Bigger Picture* objective, students are exposed to the range of voices and perspectives that exist literally in the same room with them. They experience firsthand the exhilaration that comes from the creative process and how diversity makes it all so much more interesting and productive. And, with the creation of a Class Anthology, students will understand how different perspectives, put together, become greater than a sum of their individual parts.

A Creative Environment
for Writing

While much has already gone into setting up a creative environment in the classroom, this portion of the program, as it shifts its focus to writing poetry, will have its fair share of teachable moments; not only will it help students develop a greater facility with poetry, but it also will continue to speak to our *Bigger Picture* purpose.

Writing poetry will come more naturally to some than others. While some will be enthusiastic, others may offer up a surprising resistance to it. These students often are ones who, for whatever reason, are not comfortable with expressing emotions; or, they may be uncomfortable with any feelings of vulnerability, particularly among their peers. Teachers do not need to be reminded that a student has a whole life and set of complex relationships outside the classroom, a homelife that may or may not foster creativity and expression.

Again, the role of the teacher here will be to create a nurturing, supportive, and safe space for all the students in the room. Recognize and validate the progress of each student, keeping in mind that some may exhibit progress more slowly than others, and that some may never find their groove. In these tougher cases, a teacher can hope that at least the seeds have been planted so that a student is aware of poetry as a potential outlet—there for him to explore on his own when he is ready and more open to it.

THE SAFE SPACE OF A WRITER'S WORKSHOP

When it comes time for students to write their own poetry, it is crucial to the overall goals of the program that sufficient classroom time be allotted to sharing these poetic creations in a way that continues to hone students' listening skills as well as their ability to analyze and interpret. A tried and true way to achieve this is by creating a workshop environment in the classroom.

For at least the first few assignments, it is ideal to keep the entire class working together as a whole, so that the teacher can better monitor students' behavior and facilitate discussion. The writer should read his poem aloud and then quietly listen without interrupting the discussion that ensues. It can be difficult for each young poet to remain silent as he listens to students struggling to find meaning—and not infrequently interpreting words and phrases in ways that are not even close to his original intention.

Guaranteed, more than a few times, a student will be tempted to jump in to clarify something or defend their choices. Knowing that this kind of intervention is against the rules, however, actually will unburden the student and allow them to just sit back and really absorb what others are saying, as tough or uncomfortable as it may be.

CLASS DISCUSSIONS: A TEACHER'S ROLE

A teacher's role at this stage cannot be overstated. Each student will have a different level of sensitivity to criticism, and just because they are quiet does not mean that they are okay with everything being said, especially if the comments from classmates start getting personal or too harsh.

First and foremost, a teacher must ensure that comments stay focused on the text—the words actually there on the page. Ultimately, the process should enable the writer to feel slightly detached from his or her own work, and be able to see it—its strengths and its weaknesses—more objectively, without having so much of a personal stake in it. Second, a teacher needs to allow for comments and criticism but also needs to move along the conversation before it becomes overwhelming for the young poet. In other words, like us all, the young poet can only take a few things in at a time—good or bad—so avoid letting any deconstruction get out of hand. Any more than 5–10 minutes on a single poem at this stage likely would be a case of diminishing returns and could even become counterproductive.

WORKING IN SMALLER GROUPS

Toward the end of the writing program, if the class size is large, it is acceptable for students to work in smaller groups for their discussion of each other's poems. However, it is not recommended that the group size ever dip below five or six; if the group is too small, the intimacy might make the writer feel cornered, and any criticism of the poem might feel too much like a personal attack. However, an appropriately smaller-sized group gives each student more time to contribute, as opposed to offering just one or two remarks during the course of a large class discussion. Furthermore, it will challenge the group to work through some of the finer points of the poem in order to create a cohesive, thorough analysis.

THE ART OF LISTENING

It is hardly novel to suggest that becoming a better listener is a key life skill. Especially in our day and age where talking heads shout at and over each other constantly in the media (and, unfortunately, at home), students need practice listening without the sense that they need to defend themselves or their position.

Through the workshop experience, students will learn that there is more to it than "I agree" and "I disagree"; rather, they—we—should always be asking ourselves this question, especially when we have some emotional investment in the task at hand: "Am I willing to listen and appreciate the points another is making, even if they are opposed to my own or when they are points I have not considered?" By listening quietly to the reactions of his or her peers, a student-writer will be learning to separate him- or herself from the speaker he or she has created in his or her poem; this exercise in self-restraint should increase his or her understanding of the nuances that go into creating a speaker and make him or her better able to assess how well he or she has done that.

A student also will see, by watching classmates cobbling together an interpretation of his or her poem, the "filters" of individual perspectives at work. The lesson learned here will transfer into an ability in the future to separate a speaker—whether the speaker of a poem or a real-life speaker in any other setting—from any kind of absolute truth, because the student will recognize every viewpoint comes from someone with a unique set of filters and limitations. That does not make the viewpoint wrong or invalid—just different. And always worth considering.

THE ART OF COMMUNICATION: PRECISION OF LANGUAGE

A greater awareness of language and the potential slippage involved in communication, the value of weighing our words carefully and trying to best articulate an idea or opinion—and then understanding that no matter how much care we put into it, the likelihood that someone might interpret it in another way—is a fundamental lesson toward understanding how all communications in all contexts actually work.

Listening to others grappling with one's own words imparts another lesson to the students: the importance of precision in language. They will carry this understanding with them for future assignments as well as future interactions in and outside the classroom—not only in terms of their own word choices, but also in terms of interpreting the words of others. The more precise we are with language, the less chance of that slippage happening; and so the need to be as precise as possible, to develop a sophisticated vocabulary that includes being adept at using figurative language, is a skill each student would do well to learn sooner rather than later in life.

THE BIGGER PICTURE

E pluribus unum—out of many, one. As students become more aware of multiple viewpoints, the possibility of multiple viewpoints, and the things that can factor into any one given interpretation, they can then feel empowered to construct their own perspective as an experience unique to them. At an age when students shy away from saying or doing anything too different from the crowd, here we have an environment where those differences are validated and, more often than not, celebrated as cool, new discoveries.

The emphasis here, then, is on the active and creative aspects of developing one's own perspective, understanding its biases and limitations, and valuing the ways others' perspectives are similar *and* different. Furthermore, it reinforces our overarching theme that multiple perspectives can be beneficial and, arguably, *necessary* for us to consider as we develop our own opinions and views. The expectation is not to adopt another's perspective; rather, it is to take in all those other individual perspectives and, out of it, create something of our own.

Creativity

To what extent can creativity be taught? This is a question that has sparked a great deal of research in education as well as business schools. Generally, a creative idea is defined as something original and useful. In this context, a creative idea should be something original, but a teacher should keep in mind that it should be original *to a middle school (or high school) student*; keep in mind this age group is still learning about clichés, and they are hearing many of those hackneyed expressions for the first time. So, when students are super excited to share an idea they have come up with all on their own—when, in fact, it is an idea that has been floating around since ancient times!—a teacher should be careful not to dampen their creative spirit by coming off as blasé or dismissive.

In terms of a creative idea being *useful*, a teacher should think of a good creative idea as one that is anchored in the text (something students can point to, rather than just something they think sounds good or is based totally on a feeling they have); and, even more important, the idea should be useful as a piece of some coherent interpretation of the poem. The idea must relate to a coherent whole. No matter how ingenious it may seem, if the idea does not get us closer to a cohesive interpretation, it is out-of-bounds.

CREATIVITY AND THE BIGGER PICTURE

Does being a more creative poet translate directly into being a more creative debater, football player, or lawyer? Granted, there is a leap that needs to occur from poetry in the classroom to any of one of these things. However, by instilling in students a respect for precision, a grounded and disciplined approach to a given task, and a willingness to take chances, the study of poetry as presented here can offer a solid foundation toward creativity in other facets of a student's life. Beyond the personal empowerment, with this experiential learning process, students should not only be tapping into their own creative spirit, but also recognizing and valuing it in others.

Writing Poems:
An Initial Exercise

Let's get started! Poetry writing poses certain challenges to anyone, as an observer and as a writer. Here is a simple, fun activity that teachers can use to ease their students into this next portion of the program. It may even provide a dose of inspiration early on for some of the classroom's budding poets.

1. Provide each student with a single tea light candle. (If school rules or logistics prohibit this, a larger single candle that the entire class can gather around will suffice.)
2. Have students stack books on their desks to get the candle closer to eye level. Students should be sitting up straight, feet on the floor, hands resting on their desks or on their laps.
3. The teacher goes around the classroom and lights candles. Set a timer for two minutes, during which time the sole task of each student is to observe the flame.
4. After two minutes, instruct students to blow out the flame. The teacher then collects the candles.
5. Set a timer for five minutes, during which time students must continuously write (not letting the pen stop moving!) about the flame. Let students know ahead of time that they will have to submit their writing so that they take this writing assignment seriously. Students' writing may employ some free association (i.e., it reminds them of their last birthday party and the candles on the cake), but the writing should try to stick closely with what they observed about the candle on their desk during those two minutes. Be sure to communicate these parameters to them ahead of time so they are fully aware of expectations in terms of fulfilling the assignment.

6. In a classroom discussion to follow, let students share their observations so everyone hears the range of reactions to this two-minute experience. (A teacher can choose to highlight noteworthy descriptive words or phrases by writing them on the board.)

Writing about the flame of a candle for a full five minutes is a lot more difficult than it sounds. Students will be pushed to note the less than obvious observations, perhaps getting into the different hues of the flame or specifics about its flickering; they will be pushed to come up with some descriptive language that may not have occurred to them immediately. Some students will have a moment of inspiration, while others will look more puzzled than you have ever seen them before. Give them all a "check" on the submitted written work and let the real work (and fun) begin.

While beginnings can be a little unnerving, and students, a little unsure, there's the brighter side: a beginner's mind, once any initial insecurities or fears are allayed, is an open one. The possibilities will never be as limitless as those first steps. If given the right atmosphere, students will respond to this part of the program as an exciting time, where one is ready to make discoveries and will equally enjoy reveling in discoveries made by others venturing down the shared path.

Week 1

Haiku

The haiku, originating from Japan, consists of three lines. The first and third lines consist of five syllables; the middle line contains seven syllables. Although you may use the haiku poetic form to write about any subject matter, aspects of nature often are the focus.

By the time the students have reached middle school, they probably will have heard of the haiku, maybe even have written one of ther own. However, this poetic form is still a good place to start our own writing program for two reasons: first, it makes sense to begin with the manipulation of syllables before moving on to words and stanzas; second, now that students have become so much better versed in poetry, they understand the true challenge is to say something *meaningful* with so few words. In fact, by the end of the program, many students likely will remark that the haiku—though the shortest—was one of the most challenging poems to write.

STUDENT EXAMPLES

Haiku
A haiku is five
syllables, then seven, then
five again, to end.

Spirit
The light in my eyes
could make a spirit shout out
God's very own joy.

Sosa, sixty-six
Ball meets bat with crack
soaring over Wrigley Field
Sosa, sixty-six.

Cycle
The light and dark clouds,
the way the rain drops from them.
How they disappear . . .

Pink Cookies I
I love pink cookies
Pink cookies in a big bag
Pink cookies taste good.

The "Pink Cookies" haiku featured here was the first of several other "Pink Cookies" poems—one for every style assigned—written by the same student. It became an added highlight each week to hear the new "Pink Cookies" poem of the week, and it also captivated the rest of the class; each week, the students were eager to see how the same subject could be expressed in a new poetic form. To the effect the Pink Cookies poems had on the class, one of the other students even incorporated a reference to the poems and their author into one of his own poems (see "The Pastry Baker" list poem). The allusion was a nice way of validating the "Pink Cookies" author and his poems, and also reflecting how everyone in the class was feeling as if they were in this thing together.

Taking inspiration from this "Pink Cookies" phenomenon, toward the end of the program, a teacher might consider having students write a few different kinds of poems—perhaps three or four of the poetic forms they will then be familiar with—that all use the same subject.

Week 2

Cinquain

The cinquain consists of five lines. Like the haiku, the cinquain has a structure that focuses on the number of syllables in each line: 2, 4, 6, 8, and 2, respectively.

Because this poetic form simply is building on the haiku form, it works well as a second-week assignment, as students are still getting comfortable with the idea of expressing themselves and doing so within a given structure. Keep in mind that, although students may by this time seem rather comfortable exchanging ideas about others' work, writing poems is a different kind of expression, in which they may be sensing a new kind of vulnerability. Therefore, particularly in the beginning weeks of the writing program, what is most essential (more than the originality of their expressions or their adherence to the rules for a particular format) is that the student feels as if the classroom is a safe place to reveal something of him- or herself.

Here's where the *Bigger Picture* comes into play once again: there is ample research that suggests a "safe" environment where someone knows their contributions will be respected and not ridiculed or penalized, and the development of trust within a group, are absolutely key whenever the goal is creativity. Though the research mostly focuses on adults in the workplace, the world of the classroom mirrors the world we all inhabit: what is true for adults also is true for our students.

STUDENT EXAMPLES

Cinquain

First two,
then four and six.

Then after that there will
be eight syllables and then back
to two.

Trees

I look
upon the trees . . .
They all swing back and forth
with such ease, like a cradle in
the breeze.

The Swimming Hole

Clean, cold
Warm sun on rocks
Rushing mountain water
                Skipping smooth stones, swimming, diving
Cooling

Tibet

Tibet
the yaks,
the snow leopards,
all the Buddhist temples,
all the birds in the blue yonder:
Dream-land.

Week 3

Tanka

Following in the same spirit of the haiku and cinquain, the tanka also is based on a syllabic structure. It might be helpful to think of a tanka as an extended haiku: the first and third lines, like the haiku, consist of five syllables each; the second line has seven syllables—just like the haiku. What's new: the tanka has a fourth and fifth line, each seven syllables.

For the same reason the cinquain was a good assignment to follow the haiku, the tanka is ideal as the next poem to assign in this program: it allows a class to continue building on a structure that feels a bit familiar and comfortable, with a little room to stretch. Assigning each week a format that builds on the previous week is an effective way to develop students' self-confidence—essential in any creative expression.

Now a few weeks into the writing portion of the program, a teacher likely will start to see students getting more excited or eager to share their poems with their classmates . . . and more curious to hear what their friends have constructed using the same poetic form.

STUDENT EXAMPLES

The World Below
As I view the world
from a modern airliner
I think to myself,
I can see the world below
as if I ruled it like God.

Winter Coldness

Outside it is cold.
White snowflakes are falling fast,
The pond is frozen,
I long to ski and sled now.
Oh! Winter has come again.

Week 4

Event Poem

In an event poem, the challenge is to take an ordinary object and then come up with imaginative descriptions and uses. For our purpose, the suggested form takes the shape of a five-item list: lines 1–3 offer three inventive ways to use the object; line 4 describes the object's appearance; line 5 describes how the object feels to touch. Note that the lines are written in the imperative, as if to direct the reader in his own experience of the object.

The event poem assignment reinforces what students have been practicing all along: seeing beyond the first glimpse, looking for alternative perspectives and meanings. How wonderful it is to think of a new (and funny) way of using popcorn! Now the poems begin to get more elaborate and require more description. What is especially nice about using this form is that it also requires the students to think as much about action and verbs as it does adjectives. It teaches them to more carefully choose their words, in order to most effectively "pack a punch"; it also gets students thinking more about sensory language and original metaphors.

Although the event poem is not a frequently used poetic form, it works wonders as an exercise in inventive thinking, and is placed for this reason at this juncture of the program—students have just begun to find their poetry legs, but the more sophisticated forms (requiring more elaborate figurative language) have yet to be assigned.

STUDENT EXAMPLES

Rice Krispies Treats

1. Make a big batch of *Rice Krispies* treats and glue them together to use as a basketball.

2. Make another batch and shape it into a vest; put it in the freezer until it is hard enough to wear without breaking.
3. Build a car out of a bunch of treats and drive it to Hershey park so that you can drive it into a chocolate river.
4. Look at a treat: it looks like a demolished paper cup that someone tries to put back together.
5. Feel the treat: it feels like a bunch of potholes in New York City.

Popcorn

Grind up popcorn and use it as dishwashing detergent.

Wet the popcorn and throw it at your friends.

Glue your popcorn together to build a popcorn house.

Look at the popcorn: it looks like crumpled up candy wrappers.

Feel the popcorn: it feels like Styrofoam you find in a moving box.

Week 5

List Poem

The list poem comes in different shapes and sizes but, at its core, it takes the familiar structure of an ordinary list—a list of people, things, or events, and their characteristics. It can be any length; it can use end rhymes, but it does not have to use rhyme.

List poems are excellent practice in developing use of descriptive language. They also challenge students to take one subject and look at it from different angles as they attempt to capture different aspects of the same person or thing. Writing can be—should be—playful at times; once students are solid on structure and have a disciplined approach to both reading and writing poetry under their belts, a teacher can loosen the reins a bit and let students see what they can do. List poems are great for this.

STUDENT EXAMPLES

The Pastry Baker

The baker arrives at the store to bake
He freshly bakes what his customers like best
He remembers that his friend Charlie likes pink cookies
He remembers not to make the black-and-white cookies too sweet for Jerry
To make the rolls tight like cigars for Kramer
He bakes the bread in a brick oven until they're crispy
Mixes the batter for all his cakes
Sells all his food in a brown bag
Cleans up all the messes made by his customers
Closes the shop at night and always comes back in the morning

A Slave's Life

You walk into the fields.
You pick the cotton.
You listen to other slaves sing, "Help me, Lord, help me."
You complain about the work.
You shall taste the whip.
You think of your family and get sad.
You wash in the water hundreds before you have used
You dream of the North saying, "I want to be there, Lord."
You sleep as much as you can.
You do it all over again.

My Room

With its dark blue carpet
With its black light
Intensifying every light object
With its walls,
smothered by posters of gigantic waves and skate-parks
With its stereo speakers making noise
so loud it puts me in a trance
The desk in my room
Covered with miscellaneous comic books and magazines
Along with last year's English papers
My antique dresser
with four different surfing calendars hanging off the knobs
And the soft, plush refuge—the bed
Which I am lying on right now
Trying to describe this room, which describes me.

Life Inside the Lap

I am swimming.
I am all wet.
But warm.
My heart beats fast.
I feel my stroke.
I feel my kick.
My heart beats faster,
while the water rushes by.
The end is near.
With two more strokes
and two more kicks.
I am there.
I have won.

Week 6

Pastoral Poem

Pastoral poems characteristically depict an imaginary, idyllic world that glorifies country life. Think of happy people, happy animals, peaceful nature—everything living in harmony. Each stanza consists of four lines, two couplets in each.

For this week's assignment, a teacher should assign just one pastoral poem but require that the poem consist of a minimum of three stanzas. Because the form will require students to employ more descriptive language than prior assignments, this will be a leap for them in their poetry writing and therefore especially challenging for some. Also, keep in mind that urban students might be additionally challenged; a Manhattan student's version of country life can be stereotypical, idealized, or downright silly. However, regardless of their exposure to forests and streams, students of various backgrounds all seem to enjoy letting their imaginations run wild with this kind of poem.

As placed in this program, the pastoral poem assignment is the first poetic form the class undertakes that *requires* end rhymes. A teacher should introduce the couplet as something new and *fun*, so that the added challenge does not seem too daunting.

STUDENT EXAMPLE

The Shepherd
Out in the mountains all covered with grass
came a young shepherd through a narrow pass.
He was guiding his flock to a pond
that was somewhere over the hills and beyond.

He was a tall and skinny teenager
for once, without his noisy pager.
He was alone, but so happy and content
and for the night, he set up his tent.

He gathered his flock in a field of clover
and sat in his tent until the night was over.
In the morning, he was ready to go on his way,
and his flock followed him throughout the day.

Week 7

Blues Poem

The blues poem is a product of the early African American experience, the call-and-response of slaves working in the fields. Each stanza consists of three lines; the three lines rhyme. The first and second lines are quite often nearly identical, perhaps with just a word or two that are different; the third line completes the idea. Language is typically very simple and often reflects difficult circumstances. However, despite the problems or sorrow a blues poem relates, there often is an overall spirit of endurance and survival that can be uplifting to readers.

Blues poetry and blues music go hand in hand. It is always a good introduction to blues poetry to play some traditional blues for students. Some suggestions, whose lyrics are still appropriate for younger ages, include these:

• "Walkin' Blues" by Robert Johnson
• "Everyday I Have the Blues" by Sam Lightnin' Hopkins
• "Hound Dog" by Jerry Leiber and Mike Stoller

A teacher might play some of the old recordings by blues legends such as Robert Johnson, B. B. King, or Bessie Smith. Early recordings, sometimes scratchy and rudimentary sounding, lend a certain authenticity to the experience. However, there also are many versions of traditional blues songs recorded by contemporary artists such as Eric Clapton, Kenny Wayne Shepherd, Jonny Lang, or Susan Tedeschi.

Whether coming from an old-school or newer artist, a few blues songs played at the start of this lesson will set the right tone for a discussion on how a writer can effectively create a voice—and, as preparation for the assignment, create a speaker of the poem. Refer back to the distinct voices of the pool players in "We Real Cool" by Gwendolyn Brooks.

A big part of the fun of this assignment for students is having an opportunity to try using language altogether different from their own day-to-day speech. They can approach it as assuming the role of a character, a speaker that cannot be confused with the writer himself. In this way, writing a blues poem also reinforces an important lesson in poetry study: the speaker of a poem is distinct from its poet. And, of course, by experiencing the challenge of writing blues poetry, students should gain a greater appreciation for this form of expression and the culture that gave it to us.

Because blues music and poetry are inextricably tied with early American history and slavery, as well as the experience of rural America, a teacher might consider building a project assignment that incorporates history, social studies, or georgraphy components. Use of music and images also makes the topic of blues poetry a good candidate for a multimedia project assignment, especially for students to explore in small groups.

STUDENT EXAMPLE

Those Sunday Night Blues
It's Sunday night, and mah homework ain't done,
It's Sunday night, and mah homework ain't done,
There's way too much, and ah've just begun.

Lookin' at the clock, it's nearin' nine,
Lookin' at the clock, it's nearin' nine,
Oh, the blues are creepin' up my spine.

Ah'll wait for tomorrow's mornin' sun,
Ah'll wait for tomorrow's mornin' sun,
And then ah'll get my homework done.

Week 8

Sestina

The sestina is six stanzas consisting of six lines each. The trick is all about the end words: each stanza utilizes the same six end words, but they appear in a rotating order. The poem concludes with a tercet (three lines), in which each line contains two of the six selected end words.

If a three-stanza pastoral poem is the first house a student has constructed on his own after learning the basic building blocks of poetry writing, the sestina is a skyscraper. To create one on one's own is quite the task, so in our program it is a group effort. Elizabeth Bishop's "Sestina" and Anthony Hecht's "Sestina d'Inverno" are two well-known poems of this type. Begin by looking at Bishop's poem; the students are already familiar with the poet from our work with "The Fish."

Before providing a definition of a sestina, a teacher should read Bishop's "Sestina" out loud to the class to see if any of the students notice a pattern. After reading it aloud, read it a second time—now, handing out to each student a copy of the poem to read along while they listen. Usually, a second time around with the words in front of them gives them the chance they need to fully grasp the challenge at hand.

First, the class must collectively decide on the end words they will be using. A teacher should offer some guidance during this initial brainstorming so that the words selected will better facilitate the construction of a long poem:

1. action verb
2. noun
3. adjective
4. action verb
5. a place
6. noun

Encourage students to be imaginative in their word choices, but also remind them that they will have to use these words together, and that the end words will be repeated quite a bit within the poem; students want to choose words that do not seem completely at odds with each other while, at the same time, offering some flexibility for creativity and fun.

Once the words have been agreed upon, a teacher divides the class into six groups, each group is responsible for one stanza. Assign each group its stanza and give the group its respective order for the six end words. This is where the "Mad Lib" aspect comes into play: each group writes its stanza without knowing what the other groups are writing. (The only thing the class agrees to ahead of time is whether to write in present or past tense.)

When the groups have finished, they each hand in their stanza to the teacher. Coming together again as a class, the teacher reads aloud the stanzas in their correct order. After reading a second time through, she should write the six end words on the board in three lines, illustrating the pair of end words as they are required for each line of the tercet. The final piece of this activity is for the class to write the the tercet together, which also provides a way for the class to tie together the preceding stanzas and give the poem some kind of resolution. With some minor editing as an option, the class can iron out any consistency problems.

The following two sestinas are the product of this classroom activity. As illustrated, by working together, students are able to create a fairly elaborate poem. Most of all, the Collective Sestina activity underscores the benefits of teamwork and allows for different voices and a range of ideas. The finished collective poem, then, is the embodiment of all this program strives to cultivate: an appreciation for poetry; dexterity with language; respect for the individual as a unique and creative being; and acknowledgment that when diverse perspectives come together, we are all better for it.

STUDENT EXAMPLES

Something More Than Tennesse
Sitting on the porch, watching birds who are singing,
in the comfort of her own house.
On this day, the sun is glorious.
Is the day young or is time just racing?
Am I in paradise or still in Tennessee?
The sadness of her heart is deep as the ocean.

Thinking about the sound of the ocean
makes her want to start singing.

She comes from Tennessee
where she lives in a farmhouse
never far from the racing
horses—they, too, are glorious.

The picture hanging on the wall is glorious.
It depicts a beautiful ocean:
the waves are racing
and when they hit the shore, they are singing.
Then she remembers past times in the house,
nestled in a green valley in Tennessee.

The family lived well in Tennessee;
the afternoons were more than glorious.
But they were moving away from the house,
their destination was the faraway ocean.
They could already hear the ocean singing—
To the shore, cars and waves racing.

As she was racing
through the state of Tennessee,
she was listening to the radio and singing.
Coming to an end, it was glorious.
Yes, she was trying to make it to the ocean
until she came upon this old, shabby house.

In the woman's house
through the pages of a book, she was racing
trying to find a picture of her ocean.
Here, in the humdrum land of Tennessee,
there was nothing so glorious
as to hear her singing.

Her singing voice filled the house.
The tone was glorious, the beat racing;
in Tennessee, she could only dream of the ocean.

Evolution
See them as they are wildly playing,
the majestic, bulky dinosaurs.
Until now, they have ruled this radiant
planet, but now they are falling—
this is no longer their utopia;
they will finally meet with extinction.

With their approaching extinction,
they will try to take action, stop playing
and save their wonderful utopia
(common sense, not usually attributed to dinosaurs).
Despite this, their reign is surely falling
for Man to make his own entrance radiant.

The children in the fields are radiant
like dinosaurs not knowing of extinction.
Had they known the universe was falling,
the children would have stopped their playing.
Sad and restless dinosaurs,
leaving Earth and giving up their utopia.

There is something wrong with this utopia.
The children, though ever-radiant
in the bright sun, are raging like dinosaurs.
Their rage could take this place to extinction;
but instead, they pour it into their playing.
They play, while toward their destiny they are falling.

Suddenly, one jumps off a cliff, screaming and falling:
a strange occurrence in such a utopia.
He lands where the other children are playing.
Their eyes are wide and radiant,
as eyes would be who are witness to extinction.
That is, if they were back when there were dinosaurs.

A herd of big, heavy dinosaurs
once were here, on this very spot falling
to their extinction
away, away from this forsaken utopia.
The sun then turned its radiant
beams onto other creatures—the children playing.

The only traces left: children playing with toy dinosaurs.
Radiant stars to the earth are perpetually falling.
How long for this utopia until it, too, meets with extinction?

Weeks 9 and 10

Free Verse

As we have learned through using the four-step method of reading poems, figurative language is the core of poetry. Through the use of similes and metaphors, the poet tries to convey ideas and emotions in an original way. Free verse allows the poet to create his own structure, sometimes incorporating characteristics from various other forms (list poems, pastoral poems, etc.).

In their first efforts at free verse of their own, it is very helpful for students to have some basic structure, a framework, to build on. While the ultimate goal is to get their confidence and skills ready for writing without a need for any prompting, first attempts should not be without a safety net.

Create a worksheet:

METAPHOR WORKSHEET

My (feeling) _____ is (a color) _____, like the (image) _____.
It (action verb) _____ at/through/on my (noun: person, place, or thing) _____, like the day (event) _____. I feel (feeling) _____, like a(n) (image) _____.

Once students have filled in the blanks, they must then develop the idea into a poem, creating line breaks and perhaps expanding on what they have written down. It is important to emphasize that the worksheet is just a launching pad (that can be modified according to the students' needs), that **additional work is necessary in order to complete the assignment**.

This lesson is also a good opportunity for the teacher to review the significance of line breaks—strong beginning and ends words, use of rhyme, and so forth. During the second week, the students should be given total freedom to create a poem on their own. (Students who feel the need to use the worksheet again as a prewriting exercise should be encouraged to do so.)

It is important for a teacher to realize that free-verse writing presents a giant leap for students; although all the reading and writing of poems up to this point has prepared our young poets, this free verse assignment is bound to be uncomfortable for most, and some will find it very difficult. This being the case, it is not unusual to see students falling back on common metaphors they have seen and heard elsewhere.

Be as lenient as possible with your students, especially during the first week. If a metaphor lacks originality or strongly reminds you of a song you heard on the radio last week, understand that students are at the crawling stage of their poetry-writing lives. It is enough that they are attending to the metaphors that are being used around them and are trying to incorporate those images and words into their own vocabulary.

STUDENT EXAMPLES

Week 9

Fear

My fears are dark, darker than
the coated bottom of a murky swamp.
It glides across all of my thoughts
like the day my friend and I lost our way
in an unknown darkness.

Joy

My joy is yellow
as the bright sun.
It lifts me up
as if I were an angel.
It holds me,
never wanting to let go.
But then it must drop me,
and I come back to earth.

Happiness

My happiness is red and green
like the Christmas holiday.

It soars through my head
like the day the Knicks got Charlie Wade,
I feel great—
like a man who just won a million dollars.

Week 10

Horror

Horror is dark,
like the field after battle.
It explodes in one's mind,
like when you are on a ship
and you know it is going to sink.
You feel scared like a soldier
running through gunfire
never knowing what will happen next
until it happens.
It is destiny that leads you.

Horror or happiness,
it doesn't matter.
Because horror
will always exist.

Those Bad Days

Bad days full of fears and worries
like the color black
like the dark and stormy nights at sea:
The waves are huge, and they are all around me.
It darkens and blocks out even the strongest sunlight.
Like the Apocalypse, the day the world will end.
I feel doomed
like a fish flopping on dry land
and miles away from the sea.

Loss

Although it is not new, the old
can shine with a dagger equal to that
of the wrath of an unknown evil,
waiting, waiting, 'til the most
crucial point to strike, striking red
death through grief, just as though
one had wired a pistol, set for
the right moment.

The pistol, however, goes undetected,
masked by a false happiness
and therefore as false as the wearer
of this hidden mask. Claiming one victim after another,
loss floods the Earth like the Great Flood
of biblical times; yet from this loss, there will be no
sudden savior.

As these student examples (all written by sixth graders) demonstrate, subject matter and tone can range from light and innocent to serious and surprisingly cynical. On the cusp of adolescence, they are beginning to think about the more serious side of life, and they are beginning to experience emotions and urges unknown to them just a few years before.

Writing poetry provides students with an opportunity to sort through these things; they are given a chance to articulate feelings and ideas that might otherwise remain unexpressed. Opportunities for self-expression are opportunities to alleviate various kinds of tension, which can be especially advantageous for students during such a pivotal time in their lives. Furthermore, the program as a whole can be an experience for them that will encourage them to seek out other outlets—healthy, constructive outlets—for expression throughout their lives.

Final Poetry Project, Class Anthology . . . and a Coffee House!

We have reached the point in the program for our young poets to craft their personal final projects. They will begin by reviewing all the poems they have written and choosing one of each form (the ones they think are their best, or can be their best with a little more work put into them). Once the poems have been selected, it is time to revise! A teacher should allow a period of two weeks for this revision process, including two full class periods during which students can get one-on-one feedback from the teacher.

The revision stage of writing cannot be emphasized enough and, whatever time constraints a teacher is facing, ample time for revision is the last place to cut a corner. The practice that students get here in being able to look at their own work objectively—down to the smallest details, such as a punctuation mark—and the extra attention to word choices, undoubtedly, will carry over into their other writing. And, after all this time absorbing different viewpoints, students will benefit from some time when they can work independently on polishing their own creations.

Every student's final poetry project gives them a chance to wrap up their experience of the program in its entirety—bringing together the various forms they have tinkered with, and also giving them a chance to show off some of those analytical skills they have been working so hard on developing. The second part of the project gives a student the opportunity to reflect on the process as a whole, and is therefore essential for the program's closure.

Create a handout with the following information:
POETRY PROJECT
Due Date:

Now that you have worked on all kinds of poems, it's time to **REVISE**. Select **one of your poems of each form** and work on making it even better! Pay particular attention to your *choice of words* (most precise?) and your use of *line breaks* and *stanza formation.*

Once you have revised the poems you are going to include in your project . . .
PART I
Title Page
Slightly above the center of the page, the title should read POETRY PROJ-ECT (all capital letters). Still centered, but toward the bottom of the page: Your name, English, Teacher's name, Due date—each on its own line.

Table of Contents
Type of Poem: "Title of Poem" (*Poem titles go in quotation marks!)
    Example: Haiku: "Mosaic"

Poems should appear in this order:

• Haiku
• Tanka
• Cinquain
• Event Poem
• List Poem
• Pastoral Poem
• Blues Poem
• Sestina (I will give you each a copy of the completed poem)
• Free Verse (poem 1)
• Free Verse (poem 2)

The Poems
Directly beneath each poem, in *black* ink, sign your name (signature). I will not accept the project if the signatures are not there.

PART II
Write a **four-paragraph essay** in which you discuss two of your poems in detail. Use the body paragraphs to discuss your choices of imagery and language (analyze your own poems!).

• *First body paragraph:* discuss the poem you think is your best.
• *Second body paragraph:* discuss which poem you found the *most difficult to write.* It *is* possible that the poem you think is your best is the same one

that gave you the most difficulty. If this is the case, use the second body paragraph to explain what made it difficult and how you overcame the obstacles.
* *Conclusion paragraph:* restate your main ideas, but also add any final comments you have about your overall experience working on the project.

CLASS ANTHOLOGY

Once the individual poetry projects are completed, everything a class needs is right there to put together a collection, a class anthology. Organize the anthology by type of poem. In addition to showcasing student poems of each form, the anthology should include definitions of the different poetic forms exemplified. And, for the finishing touch, include the class's collective sestina.

Of course, the anthology cannot contain every single poem by each student. A teacher naturally will want to select the "best" of each poetic form; in addition, be sure to include poems so that the anthology's pages exhibit the range of responses to each assigned form. Equally important to the creation of the anthology as a group effort is the teacher's asking each student to select his or her own favorite for inclusion.

Under each poem, add the signature of the student poet (easily digitally uploaded). The signatures promote a sense of ownership, of pride in their own work and creativity—with just a hint of artistic flair. Furthermore, the signatures add a nice "yearbook" touch to the finished product: the anthology will be something fun for them (and parents) to look back on, years down the line.

COFFEE HOUSE EVENT

If a teacher wants to create something a little extra special for students and family members and has the administrative support and resources to do so, she or he can use the anthology as a centerpiece for a "Poetry Coffee House" event, when parents come for coffee/tea and desserts while students read their poetry. Creating a coffee house atmosphere does not necessarily require much and can be achieved in a classroom, school gym, or even an auditorium. Candlelight or some other "mood" lighting is a nice touch, if available. Anything to add to the atmosphere—posters, jazzy music beforehand—will add to the magic. Perhaps instead of applause, a teacher can encourage the audience to respond to poems with finger-snapping à la beatnik style.

Let a small group of students take to the front of the room or stage an anthology page at a time. Each student should read aloud their own poem that appears on that particular page. Before moving on to the next poetic form, designate one of the students to first read a definition for that particular form. This introduction will help the audience better appreciate the poems they are about to hear, with the added benefit that many of the audience members will be learning some things about poetry for themselves that they did not know before the event.

The Coffee House event is a terrific way for students to share their work and achievement with each other and their families. For many, it is a time when they can express a side of themselves that might be a little different from what those around them are used to seeing or hearing. Such a genial atmosphere also provides a golden opportunity for a teacher to sneak in some practice at public speaking for the students. Most important, this event is a celebration of individuality *and* teamwork. And with family there to partici-pate, the message is all the more clear that these are things we value, even beyond school hours and classroom walls.

Other Considerations for Teachers

THE RUBRIC PITFALL

Having already acknowledged that the use of a grading rubric is essential, it is equally important to point out how crucial it is to avoid the pitfall of using a rubric where everything is broken down and weighted so explicitly that it leaves no room to reward a creative mind. Take the example of a middle school student who is just learning about different forms of poetry for the first time. This student writes a very creative, smart poem about Henry Ford inventing *the traffic jam*. On its own, it shows not only some clever insight but also some good use of rhyme and alliteration. So good, in fact, that a teacher might be tempted to think it has been copied from somewhere else.

Assuming that the teacher has not fallen into such skepticism, she or he might think that here is a student who shows some promise as a budding writer. But the way this (true) story actually ends is with the student receiving a C because the poem was not submitted in the correct format, as per the homework assignment's instructions. Actually, the story ends on an even heavier note, with the student never exploring their potential gift as a writer further. Worse than the poor grade and not receiving the encouragement and reinforcement they deserved here, this student was utterly deflated by the negative response to something they had been, at the time they wrote it and submitted it, so excited to have come up with on their own and to share with the rest of the class.

Certainly, following instructions is an important life lesson, but looking at the student holistically and remembering the multiple objectives of an assignment such as this one, remember that a misstep by a teacher, as in this case, could have long-lasting effects. Here, the teacher would have been much better off (as well as the student!) had they insisted the student revise and resubmit . . . which, actually, is how the real world works anyway.

THE PLAGIARISM PITFALLS

One final note regarding assessment, touched upon in the example above. Some students are going to surprise teachers with some pretty astute metaphors and adroit language. It is even within the realm of possibility that parents of students (particularly in competitive academic contexts, where parents are sometimes even more concerned about grades and ranks than students are) will suggest that their son's classmates have plagiarized. In these situations, it is better to give these students the benefit of the doubt rather than be quick to confront them with the possibility they have plagiarized.

When a student comes up with something that seems too polished or sophisticated, the first thought should be to offer praise and keep doubts to yourself; because if it is their own work, to be doubted will be crushing. Where you are certain the work has been plagiarized, recognize that there are two very different possible cases, especially in younger students: first, the student has copied words or lines knowingly; second, the young student, still getting a grasp on metaphorical language, has picked up an image or phrase from something they have read or a song lyric they have heard—much as a baby innocently mimics first words.

If the student did, in fact, knowingly copy someone else's work, it would be wise to have a conversation with the student outside of class discussion when you can talk about a writer's rights to their ideas and words, and how infringing on those rights can be a serious offense. Give the student an opportunity to come clean, and give them a chance to redo the assignment.

In the latter category, where a student has more innocently picked up language while still finding their own poetry-writing legs, you can address the situation more casually, perhaps in the form of a lesson built on the theme of "metaphors all around us." It can become an opportunity, without embarrassing the student by singling them out, to discuss with the entire class how images and phrases can turn into clichés when they are overused; and how poetry's metaphorical language is remarkable because it transcends the expected clichés and offers us something new and unique.

CONCERNS AND LIABILITIES

Poetry invites emotional responses, whether it is because the subject matter or tone of the poem's speaker itself is emotionally laden, or the student is identifying personally with an element of the poem. Sometimes emotional responses surface in classroom discussion; more likely, things of a more personal nature are going to show themselves in a writing assignment that will be read only by a teacher. When a student's writing turns confessional or reveals something about outside circumstances in their life, it can place the teacher in a critical position. Naturally, if there are signs of any kind of abuse, whether self-inflicted or by/to others, a teacher has a duty to report them. Do not make the mistake of dismissing the material as adolescent melodrama. Let others who are professionally trained in this specific area do the investigating and determination.

Still, there are less dangerous (however sad or muddled) emotions that become fodder for the young poets' minds. Even at such a young age, they may be experiencing their first taste of unrequited love, or jealousy toward a sibling, or frustration with parents. A teacher usually can gauge where these kinds of emotions fall on the spectrum of natural responses at this stage of life that is growing in its complexity as it unfolds. And, unless there becomes a concerning pattern of dark or troubled expression, a teacher can actually count such instances as successes, as students discovering how poetry—reading it or writing it—may serve as an outlet for them well beyond the classroom walls.

FOSTERING A SUPPORTIVE COMMUNITY *FOR YOURSELF*

A pragmatic approach to creating and implementing any new program will include gaining the support of colleagues and leadership in your workplace. On a day-to-day basis, it will be to your own advantage to share with colleagues what is happening in the classroom as well as any tangible results in the form of completed assignments and projects.

On a professional level, sharing your experiences will not only make others aware of what you are doing, but also may invite some insights from co-workers that will help make your program even more fruitful and rewarding. Their feedback and ideas may come from their own expertise in the subject matter or, if outside their usual scope, may be gleaned from their own years of teaching experience.

Other colleagues will have taught your students in the past or perhaps are teaching them in other subject areas at the same time as you are. And so, we once again light on the potential benefits of getting multiple perspectives. This time, the magic happens in the faculty lounge: a range of insights regarding a particular student's situation, strengths, and areas that have proven challenging for him or her in the past (or currently in other classes) will enable a more individualized approach to aiding a student's progress, therefore making the teacher more effective overall.

In addition to support from one's colleagues, having the support of department heads and administration can be very rewarding—it can mean getting personal and professional recognition, validating your program and your own creative process, and perhaps even buttressing against some parents' questioning a new program's worth. Even more important, though, is that support from higher-ups often opens the door to additional resources. It is often no small feat for teachers to get budget dollars for new books or an increased budget for xeroxing. Beyond this, approval by those in leadership positions can translate into support when opportunities arise in pursuing grants, or attending professional conferences or innovation-focused programs that will benefit a teacher's own ongoing development.

Conclusion

The pressures on teachers these days to cover more and more ground with their students in a limited time is enormous. No matter how much one can squeeze into a 45-minute class period, there are always at least a dozen other things the class did not get to cover (the teacher sighs). It is precisely because of this time challenge that it has become increasingly important to teach different things on different levels at the same time, whenever possible. Therefore, while teachers do their best to impart to students the requisite knowledge of mathematics and history and science and literature, we must find a way, simultaneously, to also communicate the basic tenets of humanity.

Acquiring information, although it makes society more "advanced" in some respects, does not necessarily make us more civilized. To help ensure mindful, truly civilized generations for the future, we must recognize the importance of developing a greater awareness and appreciation for the human condition; it must be recognized as a priority as high as achieving stellar SAT or ACT scores.

The classroom is a microcosm: if we want students to grow up with the motivation and ability to work together in the world, we have to teach them how to do that in the classroom first. We create a space where students experience for themselves the benefits of an environment of respect and acceptance; we allow them to experience the energy that comes from diversity. Why wait until they are already grown-up and in the work world to invest in them in this way?

Furthermore, when people do not fear possible negative reactions from their peers, they open themselves up to new ideas and areas that might otherwise have gone unexplored. In the long run, an environment of common respect and appreciation will foster a world of greater innovation. Although competition will always exist in the real world, we must begin with students in their formative years to help them see diversity as liberating rather than as something to fight against. And so, we end where we began, with Tom Wayman's metaphor of poems as plants. Let us nurture, let us allow room to grow. Let us marvel at what becomes. This is what it means to be a community.

It begins in the classroom.

Selections Licensed

IN ORDER OF APPEARANCE

About the Author

Sharon Discorfano has been a writer and educator for more than 20 years, with a MA in literature from Georgetown University and years spent teaching at prestigious schools in Austin, Houston, and New York. With her husband and their dog Galileo, she currently resides in New York, where she continues to engage with students ranging from elementary school to university level in the context of humane education and animal advocacy.

Printed in Great Britain
by Amazon